We are currently seeing a move of God among young people, who are expressing a deep desire and hunger for the 'presence' of God. Thousands are gathering all over the globe to pray and worship for extended periods of time, desperate for something more than well-produced and curated events. They are searching for an encounter with the Living God.

In this brilliant book, Charlie adds substance and insight to the essential conversation of what it means to better commune with God. Through the lens of the Cloud, the Night, the Fire and the Song, we are invited to consider and learn from past sages and mystics. Every chapter draws us deeper into the wonder and mystery of the Godhead, encouraging us to cultivate a rich awareness of God's presence in all seasons and circumstances of life. This is a beautiful and timely book.

Tim Hughes, singer songwriter and Leader of Gas St Church, Birmingham

In this gift of a book, Charlie Cleverly invites us on a spiritual journey through the rich metaphors of Cloud, Night, Fire and Song, guiding us into the lives and writings of Christian mystics across the centuries. With an accessible, immediate and grounded style, he allows their voices to speak into our modern experiences of fragmentation, anxiety, loss and noise. Through a series of encounters and spiritual exercises, we are encouraged to become charis-mystics: drawn into the practice of contemplation and the surrender to divine love.

This is both a beautiful reminder for seasoned mystics and a welcoming doorway for all who long to encounter more of the living God.

Catherine Williams, Spiritual Director and writer

Charlie Cleverly is an illuminating writer, a seasoned pastor, and an inspiring guide for anyone looking to find a deeper, more fulfilling faith. *The Cloud, the Night, the Fire and the Song* is an excellent introduction to the insights and experiences of some of the greatest Western Christian mystics. I guarantee it will leave you hungry for more!

Pete Greig, 24-7 Prayer International at Waverley Abbey, Farnham

In *The Cloud, the Night, the Fire and the Song*, Charlie Cleverly takes us on two simultaneous journeys: a journey into the heart of our humanity, and a journey into the heart of God. He invites us to encounter mystery in a culture of 'knowing', surrender in a culture of control, stillness in a culture of frenetic activity, and an acceptance of the realities of life in a culture of denial and escapism. This is a beautiful, lyrical invitation to learn from those who have gone before us, and dare to open ourselves to the expansiveness of God and of faith. A perfect book for our season.

Isabelle Hamley, Principal of Ridley Hall, Cambridge

With erudition and passion, this book masterfully unblocks wells of living water dug by mystics of old, which have been blocked and often forgotten for generations. As their waters flow through the four landscapes of Cloud, Night, Fire and Song, the reader receives both satiation for a deep spiritual thirst that is unattainable anywhere else and, paradoxically, an even deeper thirst in return. That is Charlie Cleverly's aim, and his book enables our often-over-distracted generation to tangibly experience sharp shards of heaven's eternity, piercing the human heart with healing power. A timely, powerful and compelling book that I strongly recommend.

Jitesh Patel, St Mellitus College, East Midlands

What a treasure! You have a pearl in your hands in this book. We are living in a unique season in our continent, and in this kairos time we need leaders who have met God in the midst of the mysteries and complexities of life. Charlie Cleverly gives us this gift of opening up ancient wells through Scripture and mystics who have gone before us. He is guiding us in a rich journey as a soul friend sitting alongside us. In the stillness of these words, maybe we encounter the Living God behind the Cloud, the Night, the Fire and the Song!

Sarah Breuel, Church Planter with Hopera Rome and Founder of 'Revive Europe'

In an age of increasingly jagged certainties, it is all too easy to bypass mystery in search of the siren call of control. In this book, Charlie Cleverly relights the lamp of contemplation and invites us down routes charted by the Christian mystics into deep waters of loving grace. Here the unhurried Christ is encountered without filter or pretence. Here is a beacon for our day. This is really useful stuff.

Mark Tanner, Bishop of Chester

I very much appreciated being able to read this book. 'Unblock the ancient wells' is the invitation offered by this modern-day journey into deep, but nowadays often overlooked, understandings about the art of prayer. Its pages unpack the writings of past ages, relating their wisdom to modern challenges and offering practical advice about how to access their riches. In a 24/7 existence of digital and stimulatory overload, this work asks readers to enter into a world of contemplation and stillness, silence and peace.

Michael Beasley Murray, Bishop of Bath and Wells

There are detectable signs in the world today of an increasing thirst for the presence of God, especially in places that seemed to have lost any sense of that presence or any desire for it. Into this desert, Charlie Cleverly's remarkable new book comes like a shower of welcome rain. And the great thing is that he knows how difficult and even threatening it can seem to find our way to God, especially in the affluent cultures which no longer feel any need for God. He takes us through some of the great mystics, especially Teresa and John of the Cross, who have wrestled with the mystery. And he shows us a way home through the silent darkness, in language that we can understand. He is properly insistent on the importance of emotion in prayer; and there is a beautiful meditation on the Song of Songs. He shares also some painful autobiography, which adds to the power of this remarkable book. It is not going to be easy, but, as Charlie shows us, it is possible to have a direct encounter with God, even in these godless days. You should read this book.

Fr Nick King SJ

This book is a much-needed voice in a post-pandemic world faced with spiritual exhaustion, experiential oversaturation, culture wars and mental health crises. It revives forgotten spiritual practices and invites us to 'radical stillness' in front of a crazed literal and virtual 'noise' as an act of hopeful defiance to the forces of inner fragmentation.

The language of the book is poetic and evocative. This is the author's gift to the reader. His own literary and spiritual gifts and skills are intertwined with the language of some of the luminaires of mystical spiritual literature through the history of Christianity. Charlie Cleverly's firm conviction is that these mystical and spiritual experiences are accessible to all who are willing to pursue them. The journey is countercultural, it includes silence, contemplation and interior renewal. Charlie's tone is personal and pastoral, with an openness of heart and vulnerability, as he shares his own highs and lows in spiritual experiences, including exhaustion, loss, faintness of heart and rediscovery of mystical hope.

This is an emphatic, persuasive, challenging, warm and pastoral book with academic credibility, imaginative language, mystical appeal, spiritual depth and ecumenical richness. Many on this journey, or those who consider embarking on it, will find this book a faithful companion as it guides them into deeper prayer and contemplation, spiritual formation and helps them drink from the wells whose waters are healing for the inner life.

Overall, the reading of this book is a delightful experience of its own right!

Kosta Milkov, Balkan Institute for Faith and Culture, Macedonia

Charlie Cleverly hasn't so much written a book as offered an indispensable travelling companion – one who meets us with love and wisdom, right where we are, and invites us to step further up and further in to the 'mystical' experience of God and life which our soul longs and thirsts for.

This is honest and real, as well as inviting and challenging, and I have learned so much along the way.

His four-part journey organizes so lucidly and beautifully a treasury of Christian mystical wisdom, introducing a host of inspirational figures who will start to feel like friends and mentors on the journey: the desert mothers and fathers, medieval saints, revivalists, artists, poets, musicians, protestors…

And throughout this thoroughly earthed yet heavenly exploration of everyday mysticism – Christ-centred and scriptural – there's the constant pull and draw of Love's song: towards the promise of deeper union and communion with God; towards a different way of seeing and being in the world, for such a time as this. Honest in its sorrow, ecstatic in its joy, I've no doubt it will help you, as it did me, to walk closer and closer to Home.

Brian Draper, writer and broadcast

As the water table of spiritual hunger rises globally, Charlie Cleverly cracks open the ancient jar of Christian mysticism. Acting as a seasoned guide to the compelling, often strange landscape of inner spiritual experience, he draws on a rich tradition of writings down the centuries. With refreshing open heartedness, he ushers us into a world of Cloud, Fire, Night and Song, complementing iconic imagery with helpful prayer practices. He frees mystical experience from the accusation of insularity, revealing how it has often ignited individuals' sense of mission. Lyrical, poetic and creative in its allusions, this book will speak to quiet contemplatives and exuberant charismatics alike. In an age of often surface Christianity, it will fan deeper spiritual longing and lead many 'further up and further in'.

Mark Brickman, St Aldates, Oxford

Charlie invites us to join him on a journey of deeper and more mystical faith with Christians throughout the centuries. As both an aspirational and practical guide, it is my prayer that this book will awaken in the reader a desire for these ancient primary texts that offer rich nourishment for the soul.

I really appreciate this book and will be encouraging people toward it. I can't think of anything that is as concise and accessible a survey of themes in Christian mysticism.

Shawn Swinney, Holy Trinity, Combe Down

The Cloud, the Night, the Fire and the Song

The Cloud,
the Night, the Fire
and the Song

With the mystics in the school of prayer

Charlie Cleverly

CANTERBURY
PRESS

© Charlie Cleverly 2025

Illustrations © Peronel Barnes 2025

Published in 2025 by Canterbury Press
Editorial office
3rd Floor, Invicta House,
110 Golden Lane,
London EC1Y 0TG, UK
www.canterburypress.co.uk

Canterbury Press is an imprint of Hymns Ancient & Modern Ltd
(a registered charity)

Hymns Ancient & Modern® is a registered trademark of
Hymns Ancient & Modern Ltd
13A Hellesdon Park Road, Norwich,
Norfolk NR6 5DR, UK

All rights reserved. No part of this publication may be reproduced,
stored in a retrieval system, or transmitted,
in any form or by any means, electronic, mechanical,
photocopying or otherwise, without the prior permission of
the publisher, Canterbury Press.

Charlie Cleverly has asserted his right under the Copyright, Designs and
Patents Act 1988 to be identified as the Author of this Work

Scripture quotations taken from the Holy Bible, New International Version.
Copyright © 1973, 1978, 1984, 2011 by Biblica, Inc. Used by permission of Zondervan.
All rights reserved worldwide.
Where indicated, quotations are from the King James Version (KJV);
and the English Standard Version (ESV)

British Library Cataloguing in Publication data
A catalogue record for this book is available
from the British Library

ISBN: 978 1 78622 597 9

EU GPSR Authorised Representative
LOGOS EUROPE, 9 rue Nicolas Poussin, 17000, LA ROCHELLE, France
E-mail: Contact@logoseurope.eu

Typeset by Regent Typesetting

Contents

Acknowledgements   ix
Foreword by the Rt Revd and Rt Hon. Rowan Williams   xi

Introduction: Why journey with the mystics today?   xiii

Part 1 The Cloud

1. *The Cloud of Unknowing*: 'Dear spiritual friend'   3
2. 'When you first begin, you find only darkness'   7
3. 'Never be without some sense of eternal sweetness, even in this life'   11
4. 'Sit quite still, as if slipping asleep, worn out with sobbing and sunk in sorrow'   16
5. 'Take a short word "God" or "Love"'   21
6. 'It was in this cloud that Mary experienced the many secret movements of her love'   25
7. 'Let your mind rest in the awareness of him in his naked existence, and to love and praise him for what he is in himself'   29

Part 2 The Night

1. John of the Cross: 'The Dark Night of the Soul'   37
2. Union with God in the Stillness and Darkness   44
3. Our Culture's Dark Night of the Soul   51

4	Ways through the Darkness: Healing Creativity	55
5	Ways through the Darkness: Healing Nature	62
6	Ways through the Darkness: Spiritual Friendships	68

Mid-Point Resting Place on the Journey

| 1 | Ways through the Darkness: Teresa of Avila and Finding the Still Centre | 79 |

Part 3 The Fire

1	Richard Rolle the Forerunner	95
2	Later Stories of Fire	107
3	Fire of Love – Fire of Pentecost	114
4	Fire and Love Today	118

Part 4 The Song

1	A Brief History of Song	125
2	The Mingling of Joy and Lament and Community in Song	135
3	Joining the Song of Songs	140
4	The End of Winter and the Season of Singing	146

Select Bibliography   153
Endnotes   155

This book is dedicated to my wife Anita's sister Miranda Harris, our close companion and best friend, who died in a tragic car crash in 2019. I wish so much I could talk and listen with her still. I look forward one day maybe to asking her how some of the mystical encounters related in this book are lived out in heaven

I also dedicate the book to 40 dear friends, who are planting indigenous new churches in the troubled but propitious landscape of Europe's capital cities and cultural centres, where we serve as chaplains with 'Europe Collaboration'. May the pathways explained here help you to abide in God and find rest and recovery in this wonderful but demanding journey.

Acknowledgements

I am very grateful to Peronel Barnes for kind permission to use the © illustrations from https://www.peronel.com/, where more images can be seen. Enquiries may also be emailed directly to her at artist@peronel.com. Her brilliant book *Beloved: Understanding Holy Love*, 2024, can be ordered at the same address.

Thanks go to David Shervington, Mary Matthews and Canterbury Press for your thoughtful, helpful encouragement and advice, as well as being efficient and kind at going the extra mile in the very numerous searches for clarifications and endnotes inevitable in such a book.

I'm grateful also to those who took time to comment on some of the manuscript, keeping it tender, and saving me from different false paths or pitfalls: Peter, Shawn, Kosta, Dan and Mark. I also thank all who have written endorsements for your generosity. I am so grateful too to Rowan Williams for your winsome Foreword, which was a massive encouragement to me.

I want to record my gratitude to close friends who have spoken personal words of encouragement to me at just the right moment – over a zooming glass of wine or in person: Peter, Phil, Joy, Geoffrey, Judith, Andy, John, Annie, Murray, Ard, Mary and Fiona: eternal gratitude to you all.

I also thank all my four dear children and their beloved spouses for all your companionship, kindness and love.

Thanks also to my brothers and sisters and their spouses for your affectionate love at all times.

Above all, I thank my wife Anita. We celebrate our Golden Wedding as this book goes to press. Your constant, unflagging encouragement to continue through to the end of this three-year process was so special. You 'strengthened me with raisins', wise words, cups of tea and even sometimes cake, as well as glasses of what was needful. Heartfelt thanks to you.

Foreword

by the Rt Revd and Rt Hon. Rowan Williams

What is it that God wants for us? What if, as C. S. Lewis liked to remind us, God above all wants our joy? What if God wants us to be overwhelmed with the sweetness and delight of sharing the bliss that is eternally his? The Bible certainly suggests as much, in Hebrew as in Christian Scripture; and so does the language of so much of our worship.

But here's the catch. What if that secure, fathomless joy couldn't come alive in us without a long process by which we learned, slowly, even painfully, how to tell true joy from artificial happiness? What if we had to begin by setting aside our expectations and images of joy as part of the process by which we become capable of a truer and more rooted and grounded delight, beyond anxiety, self-concern, self-defence, self-justification? The kind of joy we touch fleetingly when we're simply caught up in the unexpected.

All of this is what the great writers of the Christian contemplative tradition have tried to explore and clarify. With one voice they agree that there is no way round the devastating encounter with the loss of what we were expecting, the frustration of what we were planning. Clouds and darkness are the imagery repeatedly used, and we are urged to sit still, to let go of expectation, to hold our fantasies at arms' length and stay with the simplest words of appeal and need. Once we have begun to learn a little of this, we may just begin to see how our connectedness with God doesn't depend on feeling cheerful, being successful, being confident in the future. It's a matter of recognizing that here and now, wherever and whatever that entails, is where God is, where God has promised to be. And nothing can stop God being there; no power can separate us from the love of God in Christ Jesus, as St Paul says.

So we need to learn how to sit still; we need to learn how to wait, hands and hearts open; to take the next breath slowly and thoughtfully, and to listen for the deeply buried heartbeat of God in the centre of ourselves and the whole world. Bit by bit, this level of listening becomes more natural to us; and we become more free from the need to be in charge of everything all the time, even the need to make sense all the time. God in Christ is faithful in all his works.

'Mysticism' is such an off-putting word for so many. But it really amounts to this process of learning to listen and sit in patience, trust and expectation, free from all the compelling and seductive pictures we create for ourselves of what our joy and fulfilment might look like if it were left to us and our chaotic yearnings and fears. Start here, stay here. Be still; breathe; hope. Remember that you are the focus of an unending act of love and gift. And by God's grace, you will be on the way to joy, to communion; to song and intimacy and delight.

What Charlie does in this lovely book – simple, warm, profound – is to demystify mysticism and show how it arises from the central and most immediate aspects of faith. He introduces us to the unexpected, pithy insights of great disciples, from the early Greek Church to twelfth-century Germany and fourteenth-century England and sixteenth-century Spain, helping us to make friends with them and learn from their experience of darkness and light, waiting and rejoicing. He shows how so much of this tradition is in fact deeply akin to what is experienced in charismatic renewal, how the charismatic and the contemplative are two dimensions of the same act of surrender and hope.

This is a treasure of a book, immensely enriching for readers of any background who want to know more clearly what God wants for them so that 'in thy light, we may see light.'

The Rt Revd and Rt Hon. the Lord Williams of Oystermouth

Introduction:
Why journey with the mystics today?

Deep in our hearts, there is a longing for meaning – we might say a longing for God. This can become an ache of desire or nostalgia for something: for 'home', for the divine Someone – for his Presence. Perhaps more often the 'Divine Longing', not being responded to, fades into the background as unworkable, impossible to find room for, or forgotten amid the demands and stresses of everyday living. But the longing remains. It emerges at mountaintop times of wonder as well as in the deep valleys of the shadow of death. The fact is, on this earth, as one mystic has said: 'We are not human beings having a spiritual experience but spiritual beings having a human experience.'[1]

The mystical longing for reconnection and peace with God – to gaze on the Beauty – is there. It can be temporarily assuaged by pale substitutes – or dark distractions, but after the diversions fade the longing remains.

At the end of a long journey of 40 years of serving and working to build community in different parts of Europe's spiritually challenging continent, I was weary in my very soul. Like an old garment I felt worn or worn out. And you may feel the same at this turning time of history. The sights and sounds of war and – as it seems sometimes to me – an apparent unravelling of culture, post pandemic or sickness exhaustion, compassion fatigue and anxious generation living can overwhelm some of us, if we allow them to.

It was when I stopped all my activism and activity, in the dead of darkness and loss of meaning, that I found a buried, hidden source of hope and presence of God again. This is to me a hopeful mystery. I found a spring of mystical water that now irrigates my life and brings meaning and joy. I write to uncover this spring in a dry and thirsty land where there is often, it seems, no water.

Before the end of the past century, Karl Rahner wrote his famous sentence: 'The devout Christian of the future will either be a "mystic"

– someone who has "experienced something" – or will cease to be anything at all.'[2]

The mystics of old were some of those who experienced this 'something' of connection.

Sometimes they were unknown, but often they went into the history books as those who had transformed their century. We know their names but seldom the details of their story or beautiful writing unless we are a specialist. It is buried in the mists of time – and is sometimes too strange for us, if we are truthful. They were set apart, they were silent before God, they were holy and wise. Their lifestyle was challenging to their culture, as it is to ours, with its fasting and asceticism and visions and dreams. And yet fasting (from damaging foods and devices) is back on the menu today. And without a Vision, the people perish. And these people were visionaries.

I believe these mystics can be the most contemporary of guides. They were magnetic gatherers for ordinary and extraordinary people who recognized that society was a shipwreck and that life rafts needed to be built. People who longed for a new way of living close to God and in community joined them on the journey. Henry Nouwen was another who saw the need for this 'mysticism' today:

> To live a life that is not dominated by the desire to be relevant but is instead safely anchored in the knowledge of God's first love, we have to be mystics. A mystic is a person whose identity is deeply rooted in God's first love. If there is any focus that the Christian leader of the future will need it is the discipline of dwelling in the presence of the One who keeps asking: 'Do you love me?'[3]

The mystic life of dwelling in the loving presence of God is countercultural and is a protest – theirs is a 'Silent Cry'. This is the title of Dorothy Soelle's 2001 study of mysticism and resistance. She identifies four characteristics of the experience of mystical assurance:

- The loss of all worry; the sense that all is ultimately well with one; the peace, the harmony and the willingness to be, even though the outer conditions should remain the same.
- The sense of perceiving truths not known before that make life's mysteries lucid.
- The objective change that the world seems to undergo, making it seem 'new' and never having been seen this way before.
- The joy of intense happiness.[4]

The fact is that many have experienced these things, perhaps without naming them. I also believe this is accessible for all. Indeed, it is my conviction that 'we are all mystics'.

As Simon Critchley's recent rich and evocative exploration of the theme observes:

> Mysticism gives people the intellectual and emotional room to bring together their specific visions of the divine – and these are much more common than is usually thought – with the vast vistas of the history and geography of religion. People in their infinite variety connect around the theme of mysticism. It feeds that intense spiritual hunger that we all have, the feeling of being lost and lonely and unable to believe, combined nonetheless with a deep desire for belief, to have faith.[5]

There are many who have been aware of this kind of mystical epiphany. Some experience it in an encounter with God; some when moved by the beauty of creation, or by a significant encounter with another. In a way, there are as many other possibilities as there are people. Some are overwhelmed by mystical assurance at the time of stepping into faith, sensing that they are, as Evelyn Underhill puts it 'reborn into another world'.[6] Many are the different apprehensions of God, some outward, some inward. Some have never yet followed the Christian path, but have 'intimations of immortality' – to quote Wordsworth. For some it is as if these mystical wells have never been opened but the divine longing in humankind, made in the image of God, is there. For others, these wells opened once long ago – but they have since been blocked up by time, by care … abandoned and forgotten – overgrown with thorns. Yet a nostalgia for this presence of meaning – for encounter with the Creator of all things and our Creator – is there.

The mystics of old were people who experienced God's in-breaking presence – sometimes in overwhelming or mysterious ways. The very mystery or strangeness of this may, even in the recent past, have been enough to cause people reluctantly to close up these wells of life and turn away from them, concluding that they are just too challenging – maybe too far from our comfort zone – or at least not relevant to the suspicions of our so-called 'science based' lives.

But more recently, in a world weary of sameness, I believe there has come a new awareness of life's complexity and a new hunger for the supernatural. Tom Holland is one who has helpfully called for

Christianity not just to recycle 'soft-left liberal versions of Jesus being a nice guy', but to remember that in fact 'Christians believe that the whole fabric of the cosmos was ruptured by this strange singularity of someone who is a God and a man setting everything on its head – and to say it is supernatural is to downplay it'!

Holland adds: 'If you don't believe that, you are not really a confessional Christian. So if you believe that, it should be possible to dwell on the other strange and weird stuff that comes as part of the Christian package.'[7]

The mystic path can be 'strange stuff' – and wild or intense – it is bound at times to be thus if we think of it as an encounter with the author of Life. But it can also be quiet, peaceable, silent. I believe it is healing balm and, as such, much needed today.

Unblocking Mystical Wells

Back at the beginning of one of the earliest stories recorded in the Bible, when people were contested and harassed in the wilderness of the past, one famous strategy was to 'unblock the ancient wells'. We read that 'Isaac opened the wells that had been dug in the time of his father Abraham which the Philistines had stopped up' (Gen. 28.18).

In the journey mapped out in this book, we will unblock wells of ancient wisdom from early saints and mystics of church history.

I believe if we make the effort to dig into these mysterious, powerful stories and golden writings from the past which I call our ancient future, we will find the water of life for today.

This book will explore and uncover these ancient wells. The names we will use may be familiar to us: the 'Cloud', the 'Night', the 'Fire' and the 'Song'.

* * *

In the past, great lovers of God hammered on, dug into and broke through the 'Cloud of Unknowing'; they embraced and lived through the 'Dark Night of the Soul'; they experienced the 'Fire of Love' and learned a new Song with a hint of eternity, for living in the present.[8]

On this journey in the Cloud, the Night, the Fire and the Song, we can think of the journey of Jesus, who for so many is our great pioneer. For he became a man and clothed himself for a while in the cloud of his humanity. He travelled through the darkest night as he was separated in the agony and took on himself the sin of the whole world. He and the Father then sent upon his disciples the equipping Fire at Pentecost, before he joined again the eternal sound, the 'New Song', which is in heaven.

The seasons in Creation also echo this journey. The cloudy season of mists and mellow fruitfulness that is autumn is followed by creation's night: in the winter of dark and leafless trees and wet freezing rain, earth stands hard as iron, water like a stone. But I know that warmth and the fire of colour will return and, in the end, summer bird-song will fill the air.

These evocative names – Cloud – Night – Fire – Song – are all references to classics of Spirituality which will help us on our journey.

The 'Cloud' was experienced by people from Moses through to those on the mount of Transfiguration and beyond. *The Cloud of Unknowing* was the name given to the famous fourteenth-century exploration into the presence of God. The book has an evocative, beckoning title, ushering us into the mystery of encounter.

The author encourages us: 'Look forward, not backward. See what you still lack, not what you have already ... Your whole life now must be one of longing, if you would achieve "perfection".'[9]

This would be my encouragement to those embarking on this book: to have a life of longing. The Cloud graphically describes approaching this as follows:

> When you first begin, you find only darkness and, as it were, a 'cloud of unknowing'. For if you are to feel him or to see him in this life, it must always be in this cloud, in this darkness ... Beat away at this cloud of unknowing between you and God.

Comfort comes in the end: the author goes on to speak of 'moments in an hour when impulses to love God come, saying: "pay great attention". It is a sudden impulse and comes without warning springing up to God like some spark from the fire.'[10]

The 'Dark Night of the Soul' was the name coined by John of the Cross in the fifteenth century to describe the experience of suffering and the absence of God common to many on the journey of life. Many buffetings, bereavements, misunderstandings, attacks even, may also await the person seeking after God. In the internet age, online networks and communities can offer great comfort. But there can be sufferings, which may be amplified if they include loud online criticism or quiet 'ghosting' – both of which can provoke distress, depression and absence. We are in urgent times of struggle between life and death for some, as we see from the 37% rise in UK suicide rates between 2000 and 2022. It sometimes feels as if the whole world, a whole generation, is at risk of being plunged into darkness. John, like many mystics, is completely contemporary in helping us navigate these terrains. He helpfully taught that experiences of sadness and darkness can be a pathway to the presence of God, if we identify it and embrace it. And as we travel on this journey into God, we will encounter shafts of loving light and insight for this path and pilgrimage. Rather than pulling ourselves together and being talked out of this darkness with what amounts sometimes to a denial of it, we can live in it and learn to lean on God within it.

John writes:

> It will happen to individuals that while they are being conducted along a sublime path of dark contemplation and aridity, in which they feel lost, they will meet someone in the midst of their darkness, trials and testings who, in the style of Job's comforters, will proclaim that all this is due to melancholia, depression or temperament – or some hidden wickedness ... Such only doubles the trial of that pour soul. For as we shall say presently: God is the author of this enlightenment in the night of contemplation.[11]

This insight – to embrace or acknowledge and even welcome sadness and darkness, to look for God in it, for he is there – can change everything. We find it in the Recovery movements where acceptance is a key to recovery. As we learn a language of lament and embrace, this can in itself bring some healing.

John explains that we all at some time end up in times of darkness, but that if we will allow it, night guides us into God's presence. Because of this, he calls it a 'night more lovely than the dawn'. The painter Van Gogh said: 'I often think that the night is more alive and richly coloured than the day.' We shall see on our journey that it is in the night that we come to rely only on God and learn to lean on him more closely. It may be then that we become able to experience precious 'Union and Communion' with him.

Cloud and Darkness were Moses' experience – and also Fire.

> The glory of the Lord dwelt on Mount Sinai, and the cloud covered it ... and God called to Moses out of the midst of the cloud. Now the

appearance of the glory of the Lord was like a devouring fire on the top of the mountain ... (Ex. 24.15–18)

The fourteenth and fifteenth centuries are called the 'Golden Age of English Mysticism',[12] and living at the heart of this time was the great Richard Rolle. The opening words of his compellingly written *The Fire of Love* speak of this fire and of this holy warmth.

> I cannot tell you how surprised I was the first time my heart began to warm. It was real warmth too ... I felt as if I actually was on fire. I was astonished how the heat surged up and how this new sensation brought great and unexpected comfort ... Before the infusion of this comfort, I had never thought that we exiles could know such warmth, so sweet was the devotion that it kindled. It set my heart on fire as if a real fire was burning there.[13]

In the pages to come, we will see how this fire can come and keep on burning in us without our being consumed. In the more recent past, similar mystical experiences were recounted by people like John Wesley, who 'felt his heart strangely warmed'. Wesley was in some ways a mystic and a contemplative but brilliantly practical too. In his day, we might say that thanks to him and others, Britain was visited by Revival, a 'Reformation of Manners' affecting the whole of our history – and at the same time, saved from the bloodbath and chaos of the Revolution that was taking place at that time across the water in France. When asked what it was about his preaching that drew people from miles around in their thousands to hear him, he is famously reputed to have replied: 'I set myself on fire and people come to watch me burn.'

Another great leader, Archbishop Desmond Tutu, was one who spent hours of quiet contemplative prayer in his chapel. In my view, it was Tutu's prayerful, calming, fearless example and his role as Chair of the Truth and Reconciliation Commission that saved South Africa in the 1990s from a post-apartheid bloodbath. Contemplation is not a quietist call away from bringing justice in our world but an equipping for this great task.

He was once asked by his assistant of many years: 'What happens in your times of Silence and Contemplation? Do you feel actually in communion with God? Is it there that God speaks to you about strategy ... or that you get the ideas for Reconciliation in South Africa?'

Tutu was quiet for a moment and then replied thoughtfully: 'It is like sitting in front of a warm open fire on a cold winter's night.'[14]

THE CLOUD, THE NIGHT, THE FIRE AND THE SONG

The fire is one to sit beside for the healing, the warming and the enlarging of our hearts. But we may need to learn just to sit there.

Cloud, Night, Fire ... and then the Song. The original 'Song of Songs' is a mysterious jewel. For many, it is the pearl of great price, something to search for and find, if we can get hold of its meaning. The Song speaks of the one thing needful: Love from us to God and from God to us. On an allegorical level, the Song describes the journey of the divine romance – the nostalgia for the divine love affair that the whole of humanity is longing for. So deep and affecting is the contemplative encounter of what the Song calls 'sitting in his shade' and being 'led to his banqueting table' with his 'banner of love' being over her, that the Bride pronounces that when this happens the Winter is over and the 'season of singing' has come. It is true to say that all the mystics drew much inspiration from the Song of Songs.

In our journey we will at times arrive at an inner song of love for God: we too will experience this deep song within as part of this quiet contemplation of the beauty of God. This is the capacity to abide in, walk with and practice the presence of God in our daily activity.

The fact is, probably everyone has a song inside them – at least everyone who has not been silenced by suffering. And even in times of trouble there can be a song: songs of protest, spirituals that emerge from suffering and slavery. People sing in times of joy, in the car, in the stadium, and even in the troubles of life: as Paul and Silas did in the detention centre or prison. This was also the experience of the mystics.

John of the Cross, in the 1570s, was placed in a 6 x 10-foot cell in freezing conditions for nine cruel months because of the Spanish Inquisition. It was there in his prison that he wrote his 'Spiritual Canticle'. He was denied a Bible in these months, but he knew the Song of Songs by heart. his Canticle – which is effectively his own Song of Songs – has gone into the Spanish language as a poem of unspeakable beauty.

Richard Rolle speaks of the fact that after the Fire comes the Song:

> This is the life of the perfect man – it means ... burning in love for the creator ... experiencing, after the bitter sorrow, the sweetness of heavenly contemplation ... And thus to be taken hold of and pass through the joy of loving God to spiritual song – through contemplation to heavenly music ... to sit alone, that away from the racket, my song would flow more easily ...[15]

INTRODUCTION

Julian of Norwich tells how silent prayer itself is a 'marvellous melody of endless love':

> My understanding was lifted up into Heaven where I saw our Lord as a lord in His own house, who has called all his dearworthy servants and friends to a stately feast ... I saw him royally reign in His house, full filling it with joy and mirth ... with marvellous melody of endless love, in His own fair blessed Countenance.[16]

Her *Revelations of Divine Love* set out her insights which still enrich the world and give counsel and comfort to the burdened and perplexed. Her fourteenth-century world was as marked by aggression, insecurity and change as ours is today. Her most famous words, born of extreme personal suffering: 'All shall be well and all manner of thing shall be well' are as needed now as when she wrote them. As she writes: 'God did not say, "You shall not be afflicted", but, "You shall not be overcome".'

Some are called into this journey through experiences of being cracked open by overwhelming events of life and suffering. Others are those who might be described as being in a season of 'contentment and questing'. You are walking well and being fruitful and there is joy and purpose. But you long for more. You know there are wells to be dug and discovered within you and within God.

Dear spiritual friend (to use the words of *The Cloud of Unknowing*), I invite you to come on this journey.

Our journey will be one that leads us, for some of the time, 'into the silent land'. People following Christ have 'been singing the song of silence', as Martin Laird puts it, for centuries. He quotes John Climacus as saying:

> The friend of silence comes close to God. Meister Eckhart says: The noblest attainment in this life is to be silent and let God work and speak within. John of the Cross writes: The Father spoke one Word which was his Son, and this Word, he always speaks in eternal silence, and in silence it must be heard by the soul.[17]

There may be some difficulty for the activist or the social media-addicted person to stop at all, be still and experience quiet. Some have spoken of a kind of panic that ensues when the sound of silence falls: 'As soon as we are alone, without people to talk to, books to read, TV to watch, an inner chaos opens up in us. This chaos can be so disturbing, and so confusing we can hardly wait to get busy again.' This was the view of Henri Nouwen.[18] But in my experience, despite this initial storm of resistance, if we are prepared intentionally to go on this journey to separate ourselves silently to God and to his presence and his voice, then it is that Contemplation in his beauty becomes our home and we can soon even feel homesick without it.

'All of humankind's miseries stem from our inability to sit quietly alone in a room.'[19] We will explore what happens when we dare to do this. This need to 'sit quietly alone' seems a very contemporary view in the era of smartphones and social media. In fact, it comes from the great French philosopher and mathematician Blaise Pascal in the 1600s. Pascal also had a deep encounter with God. It was 'alone in his room' in 1654 that he had an experience of the Fire of God ('At around half past midnight – Fire!') which was so important to him that he sewed his testimony of it into the coat he was found to be wearing at his death. Unashamedly, our endeavour in this journey will be to learn how fruitful it is to 'sit quietly alone in a room'.

Accompanied by past mystics and masters of the journey, we will pause to breathe. We will be still to paint pictures of encounter. We will examine icons – signs to point us along the way. We will hear life stories and illustrations to anchor theory to practice.

I invite you to join me on this radical journey.

PART I

The Cloud

© *Peronel Barnes, 'Striation' (Awe)*

Peronel Barnes paints the beauty and the chaos of life and landscape. Here the sea and the sky meet with reflections abounding. We can see the Cloud, the Night and the Fire within the picture. In a similar way, our lives combine beauty and chaos and then make sense and turn to song.

I

The Cloud of Unknowing
'Dear spiritual friend'

My friend in God ... Dear spiritual friend

This is how the writer of the fourteenth-century book *The Cloud of Unknowing* begins the great task of showing us mysteries concerning 'seeing God'. And I address you, dear reader, in the same way.

We are embarking on a journey of meditations on mystical writings that have shaped so many people throughout history but have now often been forgotten. Sometimes they have been laid aside after a cursory reading as 'too dense' or 'too complicated'. But I believe that they can ease and heal and restore us – even in the press and stress of today's living. Immediately the writer invites us to come closer to God – challenging us to change, to move through four stages, to grow.

> Dear Spiritual friend,
> It seems to me, in my rough and ready way, that there are four states or kinds of Christian life, and they are these: Ordinary, Special, Solitary and Perfect. Three of them may be begun and ended in this life; the fourth, by the grace of God, may be begun here, but it goes on for ever in the bliss of Heaven!
>
> And just as you will notice that I have set these four in a certain sequence (Ordinary, Special, Solitary, Perfect) so I think that our Lord in his great mercy has called you in the same order and in the same way, leading you on to himself by the desire of your heart.[20]

The opening sentences of *The Cloud of Unknowing* beckon the reader onwards through ordinariness into perfection. For many today, the four categories 'Ordinary, Special, Solitary and Perfect' appear challenging: we may feel 'solitary' is a negative state – or we may resist any call that seems to separate degrees of people. But the call to perfection also becomes attractive when we understand that at its root the word means 'mature'. It is a reference no doubt to the 'be perfect' of the Sermon on the Mount. Jesus gives his arresting, life-defining invitation to be poor in spirit, to mourn, to be meek, to grow in virtues: to hunger and thirst for justice, to become pure in heart so as to see God. He invites us to become peacemakers, to know the blessing of being persecuted for righteousness' sake ... along with many practical examples. Then he concludes with the invitation: 'Be perfect as your heavenly father is perfect.' It is a uniquely original call and is echoed in these opening words of *The Cloud of Unknowing*.

So it is that we are being invited from ordinariness into a particular (or 'special') call which will lead inescapably to some aloneness and solitude. Many long for this solitude at heart. At last we are invited to travel towards being perfect, which we will only begin but never achieve this side of heaven.

For *The Cloud*, the journey to 'perfection' passes via growing the virtues of our character in order to arrive in the end at the ultimate goal of our journey, common to all mystics: Union and Communion with God. The writer takes care to define what this is and what it is not. It is to be

> eternally in heavenly bliss ... You succeed by grace in achieving what you cannot achieve by nature, that is to be united to God – in spirit, in love and in harmony with his will: You are below him, although it may be said that anyone who experiences the perfection of this activity ... by his grace you are united indivisibly with him. Nevertheless, Friend in the Spirit, though you are one with him in Grace, you are still very far below him in nature ...[21]

This is a major theme to which we will return later: this possibility is alluded to by Jesus when he says: 'Abide in me and I will abide in you' (John 15.4).

'Leading you on to Himself by your heart-felt desire ...' The writer is speaking about fanning into flame the God-given 'desire of our hearts' for the invisible, adorable, beautiful Creator all things – and suggesting that we long for him above all others.

This 'desire' is how *The Cloud* begins and this is also how it ends. In the very last paragraph of the book, after what will have been a vertiginous tour of the Cloud of God – his Absence, his Presence, his Darkness, his Shafts of Light and how to recognize his merciful consolations, with advice on how to travel energetically along this path: after all this, the writer ends the book as he or she began, quoting St Augustine: 'the life of a good Christian consists of nothing else but holy desire'.[22]

So, dear spiritual friend, I appeal to you, at the start of our journey, to decide to desire. It is likely that deep down there is a wellspring of desire in you: even if you don't feel it. Ask God to uncover it. It may have been blocked up with the rubble of circumstances. Disappointed hopes may have become like layers of concrete spread over it. But like the proverbial stopped-up spring, desire will be leaking through.

If you respond to this challenge to desire, this is already a gift of God. The fact that you are embarking on this journey is a sign that, as the Cloud author says, I think that our Lord in his great mercy has called you.

Dear friend in God, maybe it is possible to take a moment now to long for more of him, His presence and His power and His peace, bringing healing. Any who have the beginnings of this deep desire will understand that this will bring inevitable progression – from Ordinary beginner to Special. This just means someone knowing themselves called to come closer; special in the sense of 'set apart'. This in turn will lead to becoming someone who is sometimes Solitary – one who knows that still time alone and quiet with God, away from the racket, is vital to us as we journey onwards and to the God who waits to be wanted.

Paul, who was knocked off his horse in an encounter with the Creator and had mystical visions of what he called the third heaven, still concluded after many years journey through the cloud, the night, the fire and the song that 'we do not think we have arrived but press on' (Phil. 3.12). Arguably he too longed to become 'perfect as your heavenly father is perfect'.

The Cloud author is perhaps thinking of him when we read the further invitation that 'our whole life must be one of longing … in the depths of our will, put there by God'. And this longing is at the heart of mysticism:

> So go on, I beg you, with all speed. Look forward, not backward. See what you still lack, not what you have already; for that is the quickest way of getting and keeping humility. Your whole life now must be one of longing, if you are to achieve perfection. And this longing must be in the depths of your will, put there by God, with your consent. But a word of warning: he is a jealous lover, and will brook no rival; he will not work in your will if he has not sole charge; he does not ask for help, he asks for you.[23]

Loving desire and longing are at the heart of Mystics' experience. As we have seen: 'A mystic is a person whose identity is deeply rooted in God's first love.'[24]

How do we cultivate this first love? One answer the mystics discovered was through Contemplation.

Desire, Mystery, Contemplation. These three themes are like transportation on the journey we are embarking on. They are like a car, a train and airplane all fuelled by love in a divine direction.

As we end this first meditation, a word about contemplation and how to define it. As we have seen, the contemplative activist Desmond Tutu defined contemplation like this: 'It is like sitting in front of a warm open fire on a cold winter's night.'

The Cloud puts it like this:

> Lift up your heart towards God with a humble stirring of love, and think of himself, not of any good to be gained from him. See too that you refuse to think of anything other but him, so that nothing acts in your intellect but God himself. And do what you can to forget all of God's actions ... But leave them alone and pay no heed to them. This is the work that pleases God most. All the saints and angels rejoice in this work and hasten to help it. All the devils are furious at what you are doing and try to frustrate it. All people on earth are marvellously helped by this work in ways you do not know.[25]

As this first meditation closes, I invite you in these days to spend some time yourself 'sitting in front of the fire' ... 'lifting up your heart towards God with a humble stirring of love ...'

2

'When you first begin, you find only darkness'

Some commentators believe that the author of *The Cloud* was a woman from the 1400s, who served as a spiritual mother and director. Though no one truly knows who the anonymous author was, I believe there is some textual and historical evidence to support female authorship.[26] If so, like the many women in the past who have made huge contributions but have been sadly un-remembered, this author has made a profound impact upon the spiritual lives of millions of readers over the centuries. Near the start, we read:

> When you first begin, you find only darkness and, as it were, a 'cloud of unknowing'. … When I say darkness, I mean an absence of knowing in the sense that everything is dark to you, because you cannot see it with your mind's eye. For this reason, it is not a cloud in the air – but a cloud of unknowing that is between you and God … Beat away at this cloud of unknowing between you and God with that sharp dart of longing love … Perfect humility is gazing on the love of God himself before whom all nature trembles, all scholars are fools and angels are blind.[27]

Today 'the cloud' is a modern miracle, as in the sentence: 'I keep all my photos in the cloud' or 'I'm backed up in the cloud'. But that cloud is a tiny fraction of the power of the cloud we are thinking of here: *the* Cloud – which is rather the Cloud of Clouds. The Cloud of God's presence – the real deal, not the virtual world. The Cloud where God appears at vital moments throughout history, when communities of people want to follow and know God. In the story of liberation from slavery, which is the book of Exodus, we read:

> And the Lord went before them by day in a pillar of cloud to lead them along the way, and by night in a pillar of fire to give them light, that they might travel by day and by night. (Ex. 13.21)

In the recorded stories about Jesus, that same shining cloud of God's presence was visible when his friends Peter, James and John lost sight of their beloved companion while he was 'transfigured' before them. There for a moment the veil or cloud of his humanity was drawn back and he was seen in all his glory.

The Cloud is something those who have sought God in silence have spoken about again and again. Paul concludes that it somehow describes the whole drama of the Exodus story. He notes: 'I do not want you to be unaware, brothers, that our fathers were all under the cloud ... and all were baptized into Moses in the cloud and in the sea' (1 Cor. 10.1).

This mysterious, evocative phrase probably refers to the crossing of the Red Sea. Later, Moses' assistant Joshua became more familiar with the Cloud, as the example in Exodus 33:

> Now Moses used to take the tent and pitch it outside the camp, far off from the camp, and he called it the tent of meeting ... When Moses entered the tent, the pillar of cloud would descend and stand at the entrance of the tent, and the LORD would speak with Moses. (Ex. 33.7)

> Thus the LORD used to speak to Moses face to face, as a man speaks to his friend. When Moses turned again into the camp, his assistant Joshua the son of Nun, a young man, would not depart from the tent. (Ex. 33.11)

In the journey to encounter God, the 'Holy Longing' for More, for the silent presence of God, consider and imagine this *mysterious cloud* surrounding the presence of God. It represents both the glory and the dark presence of God.

It's worth asking: What did Joshua do in this cloudy, fiery place? Why did he not leave the tent of meeting?

I believe he is a forerunner of all those through all time who long to come into the presence and know the Divine Mystery; those who, like Mary at Bethany gazing on Jesus, choose the 'better part' – the 'one thing needful' – before all our other activity.

Joshua of course accomplished much: the crossing of the Jordan on dry ground, the tumbling down of the walls of Jericho, the entering into

'WHEN YOU FIRST BEGIN, YOU FIND ONLY DARKNESS'

the promised land, to name but three of his exploits. As we shall see, this call to contemplate is not a quietist avoidance of action; rather it is a repeated equipping encounter for Life.

But first, Joshua stayed in the cloud, and contemplated God:

> find only darkness and, as it were, a cloud of unknowing. You don't know what this means except you will feel a simple steadfast intention reaching out towards God ... Whatever you do, this darkness and this cloud are between you and your God and hold you back from seeing him clearly by the light of your reason and from experiencing him in the sweetness of your feelings.
>
> Reconcile yourself to wait in this darkness as long as is necessary, but still go on longing after him whom you love.[28]

The writer asks us to long for God in the darkness. Darkness and night can mean the apparent absence of God, our despair, the agony of humanity, other people's suffering or ours, our blindness and uncertainty about the way forward. When talking with my spiritual director about the sudden tragic death of my sister-in-law (my and particularly my wife's closest female friend) in a car crash and the sense of dark loss for her whole family, he would say to me: 'Look for God in the darkness, for he is there.' Even in times of loss and suffering, we can sit with God and be aware of His presence. 'Look for God in the suffering, for he is there.' But often we do not sit – we distract ourselves with activity, and this can be the beginning of the death of the spiritual life.

In the darkness, there is the presence. As we have seen, we are led forward into more awareness:

> if you work hard at it, I believe through God's mercy you will achieve this very thing (to feel him in this life). Beat away at this cloud of unknowing between you and God with that sharp dart of longing love.[29]

How do we 'beat away at it'? As I engage with people on this theme, the often-repeated question is: 'Yes but how can I concentrate, be still, not be distracted by a thousand things? Even if I am physically present, I find I am often thinking of other things, writing lists or simply sleeping!'

'Work hard at it,' says the Cloud. In this great endeavour, it is true we will be given help: The Cloud says, 'we will be given "shafts of light, like sparks springing up from a fire"'. With this help, I believe we can 'work hard at it', as the writer says, by strengthening our muscles of contemplation and being present. As a weightlifter grows by exercising, so we grow our muscles of stillness and contemplation.

One way to grow stronger is to use the ancient skill of the *'Prayer of Recollection'*. Be still before God for five minutes and 'collect back home' all your roaming thoughts. This brings healing. Thoughts fly away in different directions: exercise your muscles of collecting them all home again. Recognize and acknowledge thoughts and feelings without judging them good or bad. Sit with your feet on the ground, feeling it beneath you. We begin to be still, present, quiet in the silence and we may find our hearts strangely warmed. We may in this time, hear the 'sound of sheer silence' where God is. This act of growing the muscles of being present, which can be called the Prayer of Recollection, is what I would call the beginning of 'Christian Mindfulness'. We'll return to a discussion of this later.

3

'Never be without some sense of eternal sweetness, even in this life'

If any person were so refashioned by the grace of God that he heeded every impulse of his will, he would never be without some sense of eternal sweetness, even in this life …

So do not be surprised if I urge you on. It is this very thing that man would be doing today if he had not sinned … For this was manmade …

It is by constantly heeding and attending to this very thing that a person gets more free from sin and nearer to God.

So be very careful how you spend this time. There is nothing more precious …

Pay great attention to this work of grace within your soul. It is like a sudden impulse and comes without warning, springing up to God like some spark from the fire. A number of such impulses arise in one brief hour … In one such flash, the soul may completely 'forget the world'. Yet almost as quickly relapse … And as fast again it may rekindle.[30]

'Some sense of eternal sweetness' is what the writer seems to have experienced. In our drab, often urban, concrete existence this is what we need! Here there is the 'spark from the fire', prayer shooting upwards from the fire burning within; this is the upward call of God that is to be heeded. This is encouragement that God provides the energy in order to know him. This is a version of the Christian teaching that as soon as we strain to pray and be in God's presence he comes to our aid: 'The Holy Spirit helps us in our weakness' (Rom. 8), as Paul puts it. This makes the journey an adventure and lifts the contemplative away from merely working in their own strength and out of their own effort. That is to say, the work and effort required is to learn to recognize God's presence, the 'movement' of his calling in each situation,[31] and to respond.

For this, the writer urges us to get positioned in a place of quiet and to become very attentive to any spark of fire springing up. She knows, it seems, this 'taste of eternal sweetness, even in this life'. She speaks of the fact that 'Perfect humility is gazing on the love of God himself before whom all nature trembles, all scholars are fools and angels are blind.'[32]

So we recognize the movement that comes from God and the need to stay with it and grow in the grace of contemplation through it:

> Work away then, with all speed ... At such a time, he may perhaps send out a shaft of spiritual light which pierces this cloud of unknowing and shows you some of his secrets ... then you will feel your affection flame with the fire of his love – more than I can possibly say.[33]

Within this *Cloud of Unknowing*, which is the presence of God, there is a twofold experience: we are given a spark of fire, spirit-inspired upward attention to God and movement of real connection. Then for the writer there are also times of Epiphany, of revelation when there is a 'shaft of spiritual light which pierces this cloud of unknowing and shows you some of his secrets'. Dear spiritual friend, be attentive to Epiphany and 'Revelations of Divine Love', to use Julian of Norwich's phrase. We may see these things 'spiritually', but we will be granted grace to see them nevertheless. Thus prayer is not empty, but full; and after being blinded by the light of God comes a capacity to see.

Epiphanies fascinate me and I have charted elsewhere their influence through some of the history of the people of God:[34] I think they are another name for mystical encounter. Whether it is Mother Theresa's vision on a bus to Darjeeling in 1946 calling her to invent the Missionaries of Charity, or my own more mundane 'sense' of the warmth and comfort of God's presence in the early morning during a time of contemplation, calling me to continue to love God with all my heart, my conviction is that epiphanies or 'shafts of spiritual light', as the Cloud puts it, come to all if we have eyes to see.

The most iconic moment that teaches us about this in the Bible is the Virgin Mary's 'Let it be to me according to your word'. She responds to the divine fire of visitation with an immediate 'Yes'.

This is a world-defining moment. It is not a repeatable experience, speaking as it does of the unique birth of the one Christians believe is the Saviour of the world. But it does stand as a perpetual and hopeful sign that God's intervention and presence are possible. The story does not tell if Mary was praying but she was completely attentive! This is maybe inevitable in the presence of the angel – and yet we can, I believe, *cultivate* attentiveness. Among many other Bible moments of 'sparks from the fire springing up' and God 'piercing the cloud and showing some of his secrets' is Abraham's encounter where he is told to '"Look towards heaven, and number the stars, if you are able to number them." Then he said to him, "So shall your offspring be." And he believed the Lord and he counted it to him as righteousness' (Gen. 15.5–6). This is followed by the cloud of 'dreadful and great darkness' and the smoking fire and flaming torch, with its continuing promise of fruitfulness despite suffering, is for his and for our future (Gen. 15.17).

Similar key moments of darkness-piercing meetings include Moses' encounter and commissioning at the burning bush; I think also of Ezekiel or John's cloudy Revelation encounters, both of them in exile and both seeing the beauty of God leading to new life. For Jesus himself there were door-opening moments at his baptism, at the Transfiguration, in the wilderness and at Gethsemane as angels attended him.

I believe that once the door of contemplation is opened, different experiences – repeated revelations – of this spark upwards and downwards become possible.

Dear spiritual friend, for those in trouble, sorrow, need, sickness, all the different adversities of life, this quietness and the 'spark of God' can be lifesaving.

Interestingly, in the Recovery movement of Alcoholics Anonymous, we find that, after different 'steps': admitting powerlessness to change an unmanageable life, asking help from a Higher Power to restore us to sanity; and then after *making a decision to turn our will and our lives over to the care of God ...*' eventually we come to step 11: 'We sought through prayer and meditation to improve our conscious contact with God as we understood him praying only for knowledge of his will for us and power to carry it out' Then step 12: 'Having had a spiritual Awakening as a result of these steps – we tried to carry this message to others and make it the guiding principle in all our affairs'.[35]

'Seeking by prayer and meditation to improve our conscious contact with God' is the subject at the heart of this book. As we engage in this, the 'spark' that comes after surrender is some kind of epiphany that is similar to the writer of the Cloud's strengthening words. As such, we can experience today the comforting power of God's transforming presence.

To enter into this reality, after the 'Prayer of Recollection' a next step can be to move to the 'Prayer of Quiet'.[36] Having collected our thoughts, we learn to sit for a further time listening to God. This is not an empty silence, but one full of God's word and irrigated by his presence.

Hans Urs von Balthasar puts it like this:

> It is possible for us to hear the word of God because God's world is open to us. We are used to the words but through hearing and contemplating the words we should try to unaccustom ourselves to them so that we can once more become aware of the gigantic implications of God addressing us ... It is a strong loud voice – yet it is also a word whispered in the night, soft and alluring, a mystery incredible even to the strongest faith. For this voice that breathes from eternity whispers and breathes right through everything that exists in the world.[37]

Here is one contemplative writer beckoning us to 'unaccustom ourselves' to familiar words in order to hear a Voice breathing through everything that exists in the world.

© *Peronel Barnes, Scattered Senses*

Peronel depicts the 'scattered senses' that many experience as they approach silence and contemplation. We can maybe glimpse the sails of ships or swooping birds on the seascape. We can ask the Lord of creation to say: '"Peace be still" upon our own scattered senses.'

4

'Sit quite still, as if slipping asleep, worn out with sobbing and sunk in sorrow'

To be quiet and attentive can be challenging. Depending on our life circumstances, some people embarking on the journey of desire, mystical encounter and Contemplation will be overtaken by low feelings of sadness, sorrow and pain.

Often these will be so disturbing as to short-circuit our progress and bring the journey to a premature end. We are brought low and to sit quiet feels dangerous – we may become anxious. In this case, our reflex may be to get up and get moving: anything to distract us from the pain.

This pain may be sadness over our life circumstances – separations, bereavements, disappointments and a bitter sense of loss. It may be sorrow and regrets before God over past behaviour, actions and decisions. In addition, many people feel the travail and sadness of the groaning creation: anxiety concerning our planet – wars and ecological pangs and agonies. Sadness can come concerning culture: in Europe, it may be groaning travail at entering what seems like a post-Christian season of exile. I live in hope that this season is in fact pre-Christian – a time of desolation or darkness before the dawn of renewal and restoration.

Mystical writers all speak of such sorrows. This is one reason I find them so contemporary and so needed today. I believe the last thing our culture needs is a triumphalist message that denies or papers over suffering with a thin veneer of cheerfulness. What the circumstances demand is rather communities who understand, live and preach a practice of Lamentation in the midst of disarray. If we find ourselves overwhelmed, by the rivers of Babylon, let us learn from the psalmist to be a people who sit down there and weep. I believe that in the end, strong consolation – help from God – is coming and will come. But in the meantime we may need to learn from the mystics this capacity to express sorrow.

The Cloud of Unknowing feels, and is, eloquent about sorrow. Here is one such passage:

> This sorrow, if truly understood, is full of holy desire, otherwise no one living on earth could endure it ... Sit quite still, as if slipping sleep, worn out with sobbing and sunk in sorrow.
> This is true sorrow. Blessed is (s)he who achieves such sorrow.[38]

In times of trial, I have found this helpful. Jesus' beautiful words: 'Blessed are those who mourn' are part of the mystic's journey.

For the Cloud writer the sorrow is over grieving God because of sin. The closer the writer gets to God the more aware they are of sin, which she or he calls 'a foul stinking lump'. Today it is rare to meet someone who has this unfashionable sorrow – but we can pray for it. The sorrowful contemporary darkness of many today is over circumstances. For those cast low, the darkness of depression can be there as a threatening shadow. Whatever the cause, the insights of the fourteenth-century German mystic, Johannes Tauler, are helpful. He called these sufferings *strange myrrh*:

> Now there is one kind of very bitter myrrh that God gives: interior affliction and darkness. Such people have astounding sufferings: strange myrrh.

Johannes Tauler lived through climate change, the Black Death, wars and severe persecutions of the Jews. As well as these trial and pains, it was people's inner dereliction that drew his attention. He thought that sometimes people 'avoid the myrrh' through analysing their mistakes or lamenting their bad luck – but with acceptance and surrender, he said,

> there grows a precious wisp of smoke, a kernel of costly incense ... When the fire envelops this kernel, it releases the fragrance that was imprisoned so that it escapes and turns into a fine fragrance ... The fire of a person's burning love for God contained in prayer releases fragrance – the really fine fragrance of holy devotion. When this happens forget about praying aloud.[39]

I have found this insight helpful and purposeful. It speaks of a mourning that can be blessed. It reminds me of what the apostle Paul says when he pictures the sufferings of the Church in Corinth as 'the aroma of

Christ', saying: 'He always leads us in triumphal procession and through us spreads the fragrance of the knowledge of him everywhere' (2 Cor. 2.14). I think also of the drama of Revelation, where we read that 'the angel was given incense to offer with the prayers of all the saints ... and the smoke of the incense, with the prayers of the saints, rose before God' (Rev. 8.3–4).

One way to be strengthened in our capacity to sit through these times of trial is to adopt what I have come to understand as 'Christian Mindfulness'. It is a practice similar to contemplation and carries great healing properties.

A few years ago I attended the annual lecture of the college of Canons of Christ Church Cathedral in Oxford. These occasions are seldom great fun, but that day I heard something that changed my life. It was a lecture by a fellow Canon, Mark Williams, Professor of Clinical Psychology at the University of Oxford, and Research Fellow and Director of the Oxford Mindfulness Centre. Mark explained to us the healing power of mindfulness and the help available to those who learn this skill to sit still and centre on the moment.

He spoke of how this helps so much those with depression – particularly reducing the risk of recurring incidents by a remarkable 50%. But he also spoke of how it can enhance wellbeing for all people, not only those who suffer from depression. Training ourselves in the art of being present and centred, he says, is like intentionally training a muscle over a period of weeks: we learn how our attention can wander away from being present in the moment and also how to bring back attentiveness. His book on the subject is subtitled: 'A practical guide to finding peace in a frantic world'.[40]

Mark often talks of finding mindfulness, now a secular discipline, in ancient practices: it was, for example, clearly an ancient Christian discipline – he himself is a Christian. He then led us in a short workshop. He taught us to sit with both feet on the ground and our palms on our knees and to be aware of the ground under us, to relax our body and 'call our thoughts home'. 'If thoughts fly off,' he said, 'don't be concerned: that is what thoughts do. Instead, learn to bring them back.'

One writer who has called a whole section of the worldwide Church to more quiet, more solitude and to 'the Ruthless Elimination of Hurry' is John Mark Comer. He helpfully examines mindfulness and concludes:

> The way the story is usually told, mindfulness is a derivative of Buddhism ... But there's a solid case that it's more Jesus than Buddha.

More Sermon on the Mount than Siddhartha. More Teresa of Avila that Thich Nhat Hahn.[41]

One of the reasons why this happened may be that our post-Christian culture can be in the throes of a reaction against Christianity, so Buddhism is in – and Christian origins are out – especially when turning a healing technique into a university discipline!

Mindfulness is a technique of deliberately focusing your attention on the present. We don't let ourselves be distracted by other thoughts constantly running through our head; we clear 'noise' from our mind. We become more self-aware. We pay attention to thoughts, feelings and sensations in that moment – without purposefully deciding whether they're good or bad, and without becoming overwhelmed or overly reactive. In short, we tune in to what's real right now. Many faith-based counsellors use mindfulness in a Christ-integrated way as a therapy tool. They believe mindfulness can be compatible with a biblical worldview, is rooted in Scripture and can focus on connecting with God.[42]

The Bible has a lot to say about calming our minds and keeping a vertical focus on the One who lovingly created us and knows us intimately. For example, the apostle Paul reminds Christians that they're called to be mindful of this and the result can even be to live with contentedness whatever the present circumstances (Phil. 4.11). Christians can be free from worry about the future (Matt. 6.25–34). Scripture teaches us to exercise control over our thoughts (2 Cor. 10.5). Paul tells us to 'be transformed' by renewing our thinking (Rom. 12.2) and Jesus explains carefully how to remain free from 'heart-trouble', as he calls it, even in times of danger (John 14.1). He wants us to discover the secret of abiding (John 15). The Bible also wants us to recognize God's presence at our centre, as in Jesus' saying, 'The kingdom of heaven is within you.' This and other sayings of Jesus, such as that about the Holy Spirit: 'He shall be with you and he shall be in you', are in my view responsible for the rediscovery of a mystical practice: 'Interior Prayer' which is often called Centring Prayer.

'Centring' or 'Interior' Prayer is also an ancient Christian practice, found for example in Teresa of Avila's *Interior Castle*, among other places. This will merit a fuller discussion, but for now it is important to say that for me this is not about elevating the self or concentration on the self; rather it reflects a growing and eventually arresting awareness of God's presence within. It is a meditation on Jesus saying about the Holy Spirit: 'I will not leave you comfortless', and, 'He shall be with you and he shall be in you'. I will write more of this at the halfway point of this book.

Mark Williams wrote to me recently saying: 'I share your instincts about the deep links between mindfulness and centring prayer.'

At any rate, since that day I have begun to adapt Mark's mindfulness exercises to Teresa of Avila's three-stage 'Centring prayer' or 'Interior Prayer': the prayer of Recollection, the prayer of Quiet and the prayer of Union. In the next sections, we turn to this comforting stage in the Cloudy journey: Union and Communion. Travelling there will involve shedding some baggage and lightening our load – including learning to use fewer words.

5

'Take a short word "God" or "Love"'

> When you feel by the grace of God that he is calling you to this work, lift up your heart to God and really mean God himself and think no other thought than him ... It all depends on your desire.
>
> A naked intention directed towards God alone is sufficient. Take a short word 'God' or 'Love'. Fix this word fast in your heart so it is always there come what may. With this word, hammer the cloud and the darkness above you. With this word you will bury all thoughts in the cloud of forgetting ...[43]

At the heart of contemplation is the capacity to use fewer words and to learn to be quiet. Jesus hints at this in his Sermon on the Mount: 'when you pray, do not heap up empty phrases like the Gentiles do. They think that they will be heard for their many words. Do not be like them' (Matt. 6.7).

I first learnt solitude and quiet before God in a thin place – a centre for silent retreat in North Wales. It was following a double bereavement: the pain, the agony really, of the death of a relationship – and the sudden death in a bike accident of my friend and personal assistant Jo ... I learnt to be quiet before God and to pray with open hands. Previously, my prayer has often been verbal – a knocking and beating on the doors of heaven and asking to change. Of course, I still believe intercessory prayer is important. The book of James says, 'you have not because you do not ask', and Jesus says, 'Ask and you will receive'. But now I was in fact lost for words and fell quiet.

Later our family experienced the death of one who was all too young to a cruel cancer, with all the sadness that ensued. Then it was that I again learnt what a lifeline it is to sit quietly alone in a room – in this case, a beautiful chapel. Again, I found that to be quiet in His presence was healing balm to myself, and I felt as if it saved my life!

I have mentioned Desmond Tutu's remark that contemplative prayer is 'like sitting in front of a warm open fire on a cold winter's night'. In those seasons of desert or winter pain and sorrow, I learnt to sit still in the pregnant quiet – at times experiencing union and communion, which we now explore. The Cloud continues:

> Take a short word 'God' or 'Love'. Fix this word fast in your heart so that it is always there come what may. With this word, hammer the cloud and the darkness above you. With this word, you will bury all thoughts in the cloud of forgetting.[44]

This 'one word only' may sound banal, but I have found it powerful. The Cloud recommends here that we use the word 'God' or 'Love'.

At that challenging time I used the word 'Beloved'. It was a looking up to God as the Lover of my soul, my Beloved. In the background were all the Song of Songs insights – 'My beloved is to me a sachet of myrrh'; 'My beloved said to me: "Arise, the winter is over, and the springtime has come"'; 'I am my beloved's, and he is mine' (2.16).[45]

But beyond all this and in the foreground was … silence.

As I listened, I heard his voice addressing the same words to me: 'Beloved'. In the background were many verses associated with this: 'You are my beloved son in whom I am well pleased'; 'Those who were not my people I will call "my people" and her who was not beloved I will call "Beloved"'. But in the foreground was quiet and sheer silence – healing silence for long stretches of time.

In the situation described above, I was rescued by going on retreat for three days: a practice I recommend to all whose life situation permits it. When back at work, I learnt to have more silence by using the simple tool of a timer on my phone for time to be silent: initially I set it for five minutes, then ten, then fifteen and so on. It stopped me from distractedly looking at my watch all the time and kept me more able to be still in the presence.

The idea of silence finds expression in the sixth-century 'Mystical Theology' of St Dionysius. This was so influential for the Cloud that the author translated some of it to make it more generally available. Here is a passage that is strong on silence:

> For the higher we soar in contemplation, the more limited become our expressions of that which is purely intelligible … when plunging into the Darkness that is above the intellect, we pass not merely into brevity of speech, but even into absolute silence of thoughts and of words … so our speech is restrained until, the entire ascent being accomplished,

we become wholly voiceless inasmuch as we are absorbed in that which is totally ineffable.[46]

'We become wholly voiceless,' says the mystic. The idea is that the lower our thoughts, the more words we use. The 'higher' or closer to God's presence we come, the more words fail us. We may be like Job, who complained and railed against his state with many words and indeed asked God to end his life, but when he at last saw him, he fell quiet and was restored.

Today there is a longing for this. Henri Nouwen writes:

Silence is the home of the word. Silence gives strength and fruitfulness to the word. We can even say that words are meant to disclose the mystery of the silence from which they come ... If a word is to bear fruit, it must be spoken from the future into the present world. The desert fathers considered their going into the silence of the desert, to be a first step into the future world. From that world, their words could bear fruit, because they could be filled with the power of God's silence.[47]

The mystic person, the contemplative is, in a way, seeking to be alone with God in the quiet. She or he has to be ruthless in eliminating distractions, even including speech.

Sometimes this seems so countercultural that, as has been hinted, it can even be compared to the desert fathers who, beginning in the third century, left society literally in order to find God in the desert. The result was that society pursued them in order to hear a word from God.

Thomas Merton writes:

Society ... was regarded by [the desert fathers] as a shipwreck, from which each single individual had to swim for his life ... These were [people] who believed that to let oneself drift along, passively accepting the tenets and values of what they knew as society, was purely and simply a disaster.[48]

Dear spiritual friend, I welcome you to come into this place of silence and the contemplation of God. It can feel like a journey to the desert. Many voices are calling for this adventure as a necessity in our wordy world.[49] It has been said that the noise of the modern world makes us deaf to the voice of God, drowning out the one input we most need. Martin Laird writes:

This ineffable reality that the word silence points to is not something we need to acquire, like a piece of software. It points to something already within us, grounding all mental processes, whether precise disciplined thinking or chaotic mental obsession.[50]

Silence is almost unknown in our media-addicted spaces. Our world seems to be distracting itself to death, and this call to be quiet, to silence, is a healing balm that brings the possibility of being

> absorbed into him so that we pass, not merely into brevity of speech, but even into absolute silence, of thoughts, as well as words ... so our speech is restrained, until ... We become wholly voiceless in as much as we are absorbed into.[51]

This *being absorbed into him* is so rich and complete a subject that it must be matter for a later chapter.

We have mentioned the first two stages of 'Interior', or 'Centring' Prayer. After the prayer of Recollection and the Prayer of Quiet, a third and final step is the prayer of Union with God. Appropriately, this takes us beyond words into the realm of loving experience and presence. Julian of Norwich says: 'the whole reason why we pray is to be united into the vision and contemplation of him to whom we pray.' The seventeenth-century French mystic Madame Guyon wrote of this:

> We now come to the ultimate stage in Christian experience: divine union. This cannot be brought about by your own experience. meditation will not bring about divine union; neither will worship, nor your devotion, nor your sacrifice. Eventually, it will take an act of God to make union a reality.[52]

We will speak more of and unpack this treasure and goal in all the next sections of our journey. For the moment, experiencing these three steps: Recollection, Listening Quiet, and then Union and Communion are recommended as a daily practice as we travel this road through the Cloud, the Night, the Fire and the Song. My experience has been that to give several minutes of silence to each one daily has been life changing.

6

'It was in this cloud that Mary experienced the many secret movements of her love'

St Luke tells us that when our Lord was in the house of Martha her sister, at the time Martha was busying herself to prepare the meal and Mary sat at his feet. And as she listened to him, she regarded neither her sister's business, even though that service was very good and holy; nor yet the excellence of his blessed body, nor the beauty of his human voice and words …

But Mary was looking at the supreme wisdom of his godhead shrouded in the dark words of his humanity.

There she sat, completely still with deep delight, and an urgent love eagerly reaching out into that high cloud of unknowing that was between her and God … It was in this cloud that Mary experienced the many secret movements of her love. Why? because this is the highest state of contemplation we can know on earth.[53]

The Cloud of Unknowing is an invitation to contemplation. Many contemplatives and mystics spend time meditating on the story of Martha, working and serving but missing the 'better part' of Mary of Bethany who is taking this crucial time to contemplate Christ.

In the passage above, Christ is seen as cloaked or shrouded inside his humanity. For the Cloud author, this was the cloud of unknowing before which Mary was sitting. In English-speaking countries at Christmas, we often sing Charles Wesley's carol 'Hark the Herald Angels Sing'. It contains the brilliant line: 'Veiled in flesh, the Godhead see – Hail the incarnate Deity.'

We may think it was during the Incarnation that Jesus was at last fully seen – in his humanity. But for the Cloud author (and apparently for Charles Wesley), during his incarnation Jesus was in fact clouded or 'veiled' in his humanity which concealed his deity so that it could only be seen with difficulty. So Mary at Bethany is seen here as sitting trying to 'see into the Cloud'. This is an encouragement to those of us who through the scriptures endeavour to see God. There is a sense in which he is always veiled.

For the *Cloud* author, the fact is that we *cannot* with our understanding and intellect see God or contemplate him. The writer feels he can only be seen or contemplated through love. And here Mary is choosing the best thing possible, the one thing needful.

Thomas Merton (1915–68) has been called the most significant figure in twentieth-century American Catholicism. His quest represented the searching of a generation. He wasn't a picture-perfect saint but a contemporary whose honesty about the problems of church and his own failures still guarantee him a wide audience. Merton writes:

> Contemplation is spiritual wonder, it is spontaneous awe at the sacredness of life, of being. It is gratitude for life, for awareness and for being. It is a vivid realization that life and being in us proceed from an invisible, transcendent and infinitely abundant Source. Contemplation is above all an awareness of the reality of that Source. It *knows* the Source … For in Contemplation, we know by unknowing. Or better, we know *beyond knowing*.
>
> Poetry, art and music have something in common with contemplative experience. But it is beyond aesthetics, beyond philosophy, beyond our knowledge systems, explanations.
>
> To enter into Contemplation, one must in a certain sense die.[54]

In his phrase 'knowing by unknowing', Merton captures an idea central to the thinking of the Cloud: that to know God we have to *go beyond beautiful ideas* or meditations about God in order to know him really. The Cloud author writes: 'In contemplative matters, the highest wisdom that man can achieve is pushed far down, so that God may be the chief worker and man do nothing but consent and submit.'[55]

This may seem mysterious and go against what we are used to in terms of meditating on scripture. We will return to this challenge in the next chapter. The fact is, it may be that during Contemplation there is a death to the intellect and a birth of love.

The *Cloud* writer puts it like this:

> All rational beings, angels and people, possessed two faculties, the power of knowing and the power of loving. To the first, to the intellect, God who made them is forever unknowable, but to the second,

to love, he is completely knowable – by every separate individual. So much so that one loving soul in itself through this life may know for themself him who is able to fill all ... Consider this: to know for oneself is endless bliss.[56]

Dear spiritual friend, we are being signposted towards 'eternal bliss' and having the flight path described to us. It is a letting go, an abandonment to divine providence, a forgetting what lies behind. God is 'unknowable to the intellect', she says. But to know through love is endless bliss:

> If you wish to enter into this cloud, to be at home in it, and take up the contemplative work of love, as I urge you to, there is something else you must do. Just as the cloud of unknowing lights above you, between you and your God, so you must fashion a cloud of forgetting beneath you, between you and every created thing ...
>   Yes, and with all due reverence, I go so far as to say that it is equally useless to think you can nourish your contemplative work by considering God's attributes, his kindness, or his dignity, or by thinking about our Lady, the angels, all the saints; or about the joys of heaven, wonderful as these will be. I believe that this kind of activity is no longer any use to you.
>   Of course, it is laudable to reflect upon God's kindness, and to love and praise him for it; yet, but it is far better to let your mind rest in the awareness of him in his naked existence, and to love and praise him for what he is in himself.[57]

This may seem contrary – exasperating, even, to our world, which so idolizes the intellect and reason. It may seem challenging to our well-loved traditions which emphasize content over experience and presence, and it may be seen as dangerous. It may run counter to our own experience so far, where some meditative practice like Lectio Divina may have been so helpful. At this point though, it is good to recall that Jesus himself said: 'You search the Scriptures because you think that in them you have eternal life, but it is they that bear witness to me' (John 5.39).

I believe, in fact, that the Cloud is here helpfully calling us to add to these precious practices of meditation on stories and images, brilliant though these can be, to go beyond them towards total loving encounter. We are called by the writer to through and beyond into a space that is challenging.

For God is completely other: He is more than a King, beyond a Shepherd, greater than a Father even ... He is beyond Light or Darkness: he is utterly other, completely beyond. In the ancient story of the prophet Elijah, God is not in the wind, not in the earthquake, not in the fire. (1 Kings 19.12)

We here border on 'apophatic theology' – or 'knowledge of God found by negation'. It is an attempt to describe God by what cannot be said about him. When we say that God is infinite, we are also saying that God is not finite – or not limited. This has links to the *via negativa* – which attempts to describe God by what he is not.

I invite you to see this as an adventure: we are travelling into the beyond. It is a journey into mystery and in the next chapter we will explore this. We are travelling 'back to the future' – or into the ancient future.

7

'Let your mind rest in the awareness of him in his naked existence, and to love and praise him for what he is in himself'

It is interesting to me that today there is such a threat to people's mental health and such a lack of peace in so many hearts that it has become a cultural norm to talk about and recommend meditation as a key to healthy living or as a key to survival. Usually this involves silence, mindfulness and being present to the moment. By this route, which does not begin so much with the study of Christ but rather begins with sickness in this world and all its noise, might people be coming to a similar destination: the presence of God in the silence? I pray God it might be so.

The other route, involving meditations on the life of Christ and his sacrifice for our sins, was completely crucial for the writer of the Cloud as the way into the spiritual life. And this has been my own journey, which I value beyond all price.

But in the end, for the writer, it is well if we can travel through these meditations and beyond them: these must be buried in the cloud of forgetting ...

This mystic calls us in the end to sit with God and hear his word. Instead of surrounding him with our words, lists, requests. Instead of reminding him of other images concerning him ... We go beyond all these to listen to his word, the 'gentle whisper' already spoken in the silence.

This is simple but costs us everything. In this sense it is a death. A death to, or a putting down of, the intellect and a birth to the faculty of love.

This is why Thomas Merton says, as we have seen: 'In contemplation we know by unknowing, or better, we know beyond knowing. To enter into contemplation, one must in a certain sense die.'

It is good to be aware that there are broadly three different strands in mysticism.[58] It is not that one is better than the rest. We may have more affinity with one or the other, but I have found that it can be creative, intriguing and healing to explore all three.

Some mystics concentrate on finding God in the divine names and the sense experiences of God's presence flowing from these. There is immense benefit in meditating on and thinking about these names. A fruitful exercise when praying through the Lord's Prayer can be to linger on the sentence 'Hallowed be thy name', and list some of the many names and the characteristics of God.[59]

Others are creation mystics, finding God in and through nature. The creation speaks of God:

> The heavens are telling the glory of God,
>   and the sky above proclaims his handiwork.
> Day to day pours out speech ...
> (Psalm 19.1–2)

These mystical contemplatives are not identifying nature with the Divine but discerning God's presence in, with and through his beautiful creation.

A third group concentrates on this *paradox of negation*. This group will include John of the Cross, Meister Eckhart, *The Cloud of Unknowing* and many others. These people are straining with a holy longing for the very presence of God but are running out of words to express it. The only expression that they can find is that God is *not* this or that attribute. These are the ones travelling down the *via negativa*.

As we have said, the sixth-century mystic who took the name Dionysius[60] was one of the inspirations for *The Cloud of Unknowing*, so much so that the author translated part of his 'Mystical Theology'. Dionysius writes in his *On the Divine Names*:

> The Sacred Writers praise the divine Origin for possessing all names, while yet they call him Nameless.
>
>   For instance ... they say that the Supreme Godhead Himself, in one of the mystical visions whereby he was manifested, rebuked him who said: 'What is thy name?' and, as though bidding him not seek by any means of any Name to acquire a knowledge of God, made the answer: 'Why do you ask thus after my Name?' ...

> Now is not the secret Name precisely that which is above all names and nameless, and is fixed beyond every name that is named, not only in this world but also in that which is to come? On the other hand, they attribute many names to It when, for instance, they speak of It as declaring: 'I am that I am.'[61]

Although pressing into this may seem challenging, this is in fact what St Augustine teaches when he says that the Prologue of St John's Gospel reveals the mysteries of Eternity not as they actually are but only as human thought can grasp them.

Moses in the cloud on the mountain had God's character revealed to him as 'slow to anger and abounding in steadfast love' (Ex. 34.6). Then Jesus in his incarnation unveiled more and more of God's Father heart, his character, his loving mercy. And he repeatedly spoke of his name, for example in John 17, saying that he has revealed it, praying that his Father may 'keep' his disciples in his name, saying later, 'I made known to them your name and will continue to make it known' (John 17.23). However, it is more likely that this means the unfailing love and the character, kindness and presence of God himself, rather than one particular 'name'. As Paul wrote to the Philippians, his is the 'name above all names' (Phil. 2.10). The word translated as 'holy' (kadosh) implies otherness, being set apart and being without sin.

Recovery movements such as Alcoholics Anonymous, which are so powerful in their effectiveness to help the addicted, express a reluctance to use the name 'God', preferring the term 'Higher Power'. Of course, this is partly done to avoid a term that comes with too many associations for some to be helpful. But the fact is, many people today find the humility and uncertainty of this description attractive and important. It is not too far from Dionysius who, grasping at this, writes in a beautiful passage:

> We therefore maintain that the universal and transcendent Cause of all things is neither ... subject to any disorder or disturbance, nor influenced by any earthly passion: he needs no light, suffers no change, corruption, division, privation, or flux ... neither can the reason attain to him, nor name him, nor know him; neither is he darkness nor light ... the all perfect and unique Cause of all things transcends all affirmation, and the simple pre-eminence of his nature is outside of every negation – free from every limitation and beyond them all.[62]

This is mysterious and 'beyond' – the 'apophatic' reaching out to God beyond our naming of him.

* * *

Dear spiritual friend, can we with the mystics rejoice in paradox? Can we enjoy word pictures like 'eloquent silence', 'filled emptiness' as being evocative, even accurate? The mystic rejoices in paradox, using ideas like 'darkness that outshines all resplendence'. Or as Meister Eckhart put it: 'there I heard without sound, there I saw without light.'[63] The writer of the Cloud yearns for what Dionysius calls God's wisdom and treasure, his 'bright darkness', his 'ignorant knowledge', saying: 'This is what makes you silent in thought as well as speech. This makes your prayer very short ... By this you are taught to forsake the world.'[64]

We stretch our vocabulary to describe him. A final stage, to conclude this first stage of our journey, is to use the image of sleep – forgetful sleep. 'Contemplation is like sleep' is another apophatic image used by the Cloud author, and we will close with this:

> This work of contemplation is rightly compared to a sleep. For as in sleep the use of your bodily senses is suspended, so that the body can rest completely, sustaining and strengthening its physical powers, just so in this sleep, the unruly questionings of the untamed spiritual senses, speculations aroused from mental images, are firmly bound and completely deprived of their force, so that the blessed soul can sleep softly and rest in loving perception of God as he is, fully strengthening and sustaining its spiritual powers.[65]

The fact is that with the advent of the internet and the culture of the instant global village newsfeed that we inhabit today, many people experience particularly steep challenges, as well as, for many, sleep challenges. The speed and pace of life have accelerated. The clamour of cultural change has increased ... The noise of social media with its likes or its 'unfriendings' has grown deafening for many. Arguably, we need great resilience and skill to navigate this new landscape, even though, for some, social network communities can be of real comfort.

But here, 600 years after its writing, might it be that *The Cloud of Unknowing* could be considered surprisingly relevant and helpful? What a comfort and strength that we are able to 'rest in loving perception of God as he is'; and the 'unruly questionings, untamed spiritual senses, speculations aroused from mental images' can, through recollection, quiet and union and communion, be 'firmly bound and completely deprived of their force'. We can 'rest sustaining and strengthening our physical powers'.[66]

Dear friend in God. I invite you therefore to have a good rest in God and to sleep well even in the place of silence that is Contemplation. This also is love and joy and peace in believing.

We have reached the end of our journey through the Cloud of Unknowing. After this, we travel into the divine dark – the dark night of the soul. And we will discover four ways to lighten our darkness on the path.

PART 2

The Night

© *Peronel Barnes, 'Weatherfront'*

The picture draws us into subtle versions of weather and at least four tones of dark. In the foreground deep darkness creeps over the land like smoke. Then it seems a choppy sea is churning. The sky seems diagonally divided into dark and light. It is as if hope is coming.

I

John of the Cross: 'The Dark Night of the Soul'

One dark night,
Fired with love's urgent longings
– Ah, the sheer grace! –
I went out unseen,
My house being now all stilled; ...

In darkness and concealment,
My house being now all stilled; ...

With no other light or guide
Than the one that burned in my heart; ... O guiding night!
O night more lovely than the dawn!
O night that has united
The lover with his beloved,
Transforming the beloved in her lover. ...
...
I abandoned and forgot myself
Laying my face on my beloved;
All things ceased; I went out from myself,
Leaving my cares
Forgotten among the lilies.
(John of the Cross, 'The Dark Night of the Soul')[67]

At times, and seemingly at the centre of so many lives, we find there lies a quiet despair, a quiet desperation.[68] It falls, like the rain, on both the just and the unjust. This 'Dark Night' haunts and prowls and overtakes people in the midst of their strength. Darkness at Noon descends on the sports icon, the pop idol, the poet and the priest – as well as the young, the teenager, the business person, the teacher, the medic. It afflicts people from the poor and the prisoner to the successful and the savvy; it can creep up stealthily in the soul of the married and the single, the brave and the bowed down alike.

Darkness perhaps draws particularly close to the bereaved, those who have lost a friend, a spouse, a parent, a child, either through death or through estrangement – that so common modern ailment that brings despair and loss of hope in its wake.

Sometimes this 'quiet desperation' is a result of poverty, war, migration and deprivation: this is the sorry state of so many in this unstable continent today, as the remarkable book of reportage *This is Europe* shows.[69] Sometimes Darkness falling has no apparent cause: it comes close just like the night comes – for no reason other than gravity.

For the seeker of God or of Goodness and of Love, Darkness also inevitably falls. The way forward is not to avoid it but to find God and goodness in the darkness, for they are there. What light can we find to guide us through?

In J. R. R. Tolkien's great trilogy of battle between darkness and light, *The Lord of the Rings*, Galadriel gives Frodo a gift saying: 'May it be a light to you in dark places.' Later in the story, Frodo's friend Sam encourages him, saying that their desperate plight

> 'is like in the great stories – the ones that really mattered. Full of darkness and danger, they were, and sometimes you did not want to know the end because how could the end be happy? How could the world go back to what it was when so much bad had happened? But in the end, it's only a passing thing, this shadow.'[70]

Tolkien was writing after the horrors of World War One. 'When I returned from the war,' he said, 'all but one of my close friends were dead.'[71] In walking through darkness, we may well need both a gift, like Galadriel's phial of light, or we may need perspective and the long view like that offered by Sam. Who can give us such gifts and perspective in the Dark Nights of the soul? For this we turn to the man who invented the term, St John of the Cross.

John lived in Central Spain in 1542–91, during the country's so-called 'Golden Age' of geographical expansion and the flowering of the Arts with giant authors like Cervantes and painters like Velasquez flourishing. He is viewed as one of the greatest mystics and Spanish poets – a Doctor of the Church, a reformer of monasticism and patron of poets and contemplatives. But in his journey bringing reform and kindness, he suffered violence, cruelty, rejection, imprisonment and illness.

JOHN OF THE CROSS: 'THE DARK NIGHT OF THE SOUL'

John's great contribution was to make sense of the feelings of brokenness, sadness and despair that can invade all of us, including those wanting to connect with God, and to give them a name in his poem 'The Dark Night of the Soul' (*La noche oscura del alma*).

I believe this great discovery is particularly relevant and needed today. The fact is that in our times the virtue of emotional intelligence or emotional awareness has been placed in what seems like a perpetual spotlight. At any rate, there is a new acknowledgment that there is so much sorrow, so much quiet desperation – including depression even – and in so many lives.

This makes John the most contemporary of companions as we approach this poignant landscape of 'the dark night'.

John was a creative whose work is unusual in that it consists mainly of commentaries that carefully explain his great poems 'The Dark Night of the Soul', 'The Spiritual Canticle' and 'The Living Flame of Love'. We will explore extracts from these jewel-like poems as we embark on the task of making sense of – and finding comfort in – this phenomenon experienced at some time by most people: the Dark Night of the Soul.

What are the sharp, dark, engulfingly sad scenarios that we may encounter in our lives? There are many, but to mention some: bereavement, estrangement, betrayal, absence of meaning, anxiety and depression, having a death wish or the desire even to end our life. For many, wars and climate disasters are part of the dark night. The American psychologist Thomas Moore states bleakly in his *Dark Nights of the Soul* that sometimes it feels like the whole planet is in a 'Dark Night'.[72]

Above all we might say that the great darkness is *a feeling of the complete absence of God – and therefore of meaninglessness.* For the spiritual person who is longing for and looking for God, this darkness is deeply alarming. John of the Cross's major theme of darkness has to do with this, in his view, essential stage on our journey to God. He speaks of *NADA! (Nothing!)* – the absence of the peace and presence of God – and many will identify with this at some point in their lives. But John, as we will see, finds this nothingness to be eventually an essential and fruitful pathway to being in the end immersed in God.

Whatever the cause, very many in our day are faced with a dark night.

We are not helping ourselves if we view feelings of despair and emptiness as a deviation from the healthy and happy life we claim as our normal state of being or even what we deserve. Jesus himself said: 'In the world you will have trouble' (John 16.33). He said: 'Blessed are those who mourn' (Matt. 5.4). Some believe it is best that we can learn to value visitations of melancholy and sadness. They can contain times of enlightenment and help us become people of insight and compassion.

All mystics speak of this. One who lived many dark nights of bereavement, an unhappy marriage and then bereavement, loss and imprisonment under Louis XIV was the seventeenth-century French mystic Jeanne Guyon, whose *Experiencing the Depths of Jesus Christ* and her *Autobiography* contain this among many insights:

> If knowing answers to life's questions is absolutely necessary to you, then forget the journey. You will never make it, for this is a journey of unknowables – of unanswered questions, enigmas, incomprehensibles, and most of all, things unfair.[73]

In *The Cloud of Unknowing* we read:

> The first time you practise contemplation, you'll only experience a darkness, like a cloud of unknowing. You won't know what it is. You'll only know that in your will you feel a simple reaching out to God. This darkness and this cloud will always keep you from seeing him clearly by the light of understanding in your intellect and will block you from feeling him fully in the sweetness of love in your emotions. So, be sure to make your home in this darkness. Stay there as long as you can, crying out to him over and over again because you love him. It's the closest you can get to God here on earth, by waiting in this darkness and in this cloud. Work at this diligently, as I've asked you to, and I know God's mercy will lead you there.[74]

The great English commentator on mysticism, Evelyn Underhill, speaks of the unavoidable journey through what she calls 'the Quiet', 'the Desert of God', and 'the Divine Dark'. She says:

> Finding yourself in this place of darkness, you are to dwell there meekly asking nothing seeking nothing, but with your doors flung wide open towards God, and there will come to you a certitude that this darkness enveils the goal that you have been seeking from the first – the final reality, the perfect satisfaction. If you are to make it through the passive suffering, a mighty transformation will result. You will be reborn into another world.[75]

JOHN OF THE CROSS: 'THE DARK NIGHT OF THE SOUL'

Dear spiritual friend, I pause to ask: do you find yourself at times enveloped in darkness? Of course we may lessen its weight by bursting into activism and distractions, but it is healthy to ask: as a constant backdrop, is there darkness? If so, at this time try settling into it to see what John can teach us.

John of the Cross's poems encourage us to see that, if we will dare to believe it, in these times of great distress, of great darkness we can, *in extremis*, learn to lean on God – we lean blindly maybe, not understanding, but lean nonetheless. In the dark night, when by definition we have no energy, we grow the muscles of holding on. Like a person thrown into the water in a great storm, we hold on to the life raft with our knuckles white and freezing. We hold on.

Part of John's own story was of an extremely dark night. In 1577, at 35 years old, he was abducted by his own monastic brothers who were opposed to his efforts to reform the Carmelite order, and imprisoned for nine months in Toledo. Mirabai Starr puts it like this: 'It was there, as he suffered, that the caterpillar of his old self dissolved and the butterfly of his authentic being grew its wings.'[76] His prison cell, a stone room hardly large enough for his body, had formerly been a toilet. His clothing – his habit – rotted from his body in the heat of summer, and in winter he shivered in the rag that remained. At different times each week the brothers brought him out to be beaten. Otherwise, he sat in the darkness, tracking the stars through the single small window high up in the wall of his cell.

Doubt began to invade his soul and, though he clung to the life-raft of faith, it began to disintegrate in his hands and he drifted into despair. Like Jonah in the belly of the fierce fish (an image John later used when he wrote the commentary to 'Dark Night of the Soul'), the imprisoned creative found himself suspended in the void. John drew at this time a picture of Christ on the cross seen dramatically from above. This image was later the inspiration for Salvador Dali's famous painting 'Christ of St John of the Cross', seen from above with planet earth below.

It was painful enough for him to wonder if God had given up on him, but more agony descended when he began to find himself giving up on God. At last, he simply ran out of energy, and it seems he let himself down into the arms of radical unknowingness – which is where, tried in the fire, his agony began to come forth as the gold of mystical poetry.[77]

John's response was to hold on to God.

This is in contrast to the response of philosophers, writers and influencers in the modern and post-modern world. The prevailing conclusion today is often to reject God, and the counsel of the wisdom of today is to live bravely without God. In my view this life without God for many only serves to increase the levels of darkness experienced in our culture today.

By contrast, John's response is to hold on. And this can be and is a way forward today in the darkness.

John holds on to God, as the former addict who has become meek and broken holds on for dear life to a Higher Power.

He believes, and hands his life over in the darkness. Like the Bride in the scripture John loved best – the Song of Songs – he went 'following the footsteps of the shepherds' and of his Beloved through the night-time streets and squares of his ravaged heart and memories (Song 1.8, 3.2ff.). Finding no trace of the One who 'wounded his soul and set it on fire', he converted his yearning into sublime, longing love-language.

His three poems 'The Dark Night,' 'Spiritual Canticle' and 'The Living Flame of Love' are John's own versions of the Song of Songs. The Song of Songs can of course be read as an earthy love story. In addition, the Church Fathers and Mystics and many interpreters to the present day have read it on an allegorical level to tell all of our stories as the betrothed bride of Christ.[78] In this interpretation of the Divine Romance, John writes of our progress from fear, uncertainty and attack from 'little foxes that ruin the vineyard' through to a place of hope and encounter where 'the winter is over'. He tells of the arrival of springtime, beauty, a season of singing, maturity, trust and, in the end, Divine Union.

The beautiful journeys described in 'The Spiritual Canticle' and 'The Dark Night' are what emerged from that imprisonment. The fruit of that alchemy sustained the poet in his imprisonment and has continued to feed the rest of us for five centuries.[79] His barren cell became a place of creativity and composition. Malcolm Guite's poem 'John of the Cross' summarizes the life we have been describing and John's journey through the darkness:

> Deep in the dark your brothers locked you up
> But not so deep as your dear Love could dive,
> There at the end of colour, sense and shape,
> The dark dead end that tells us we're alive,
> You sang aloud and found your absent lover,
> As light's true end comes with the end of light.
> In the rich midnight came the lovely other,
> You saw him plain although it was the night.

And now you call us all to hear that Fountain
Singing and playing well before the Dawn
The sun is still below this shadowed mountain
We wait in darkness for him to be born.
Before he rises, light-winged with the lark,
We'll meet with our beloved in the dark.[80]

2

Union with God in the Stillness and Darkness

One dark night,
Fired with love's urgent longings
– Ah, the sheer grace! –
I went out unseen,
My house being now all stilled.

John of the Cross begins his poem, 'One dark night'.

The first words show the darkness, the blindness, the challenge of not seeing, not understanding: 'One dark night'.

For John, darkness comes inevitably as people long for love and long for God. It is a paradox but 'The brighter the light, the more the owl is blinded; and the more one looks at the brilliant sun, the more the sun darkens the faculty of sight, deprives it and overwhelms it in its weakness.' So it is that people seeking for truth, as well as those seeking God, can feel blind and darkness can descend. John writes that this may also happen when we embark on the journey into silence and contemplation: 'when the divine light of contemplation strikes souls not entirely illumined, it causes spiritual darkness ... [and] also deprives and darkens their understanding.'[81]

He speaks, as do so many mystics, of abandoning some of our spiritual practices and even our understanding and walking into the dark night itself. He also encourages us to cease from thinking good thoughts – or maybe to stop going aside to meditate on the life of Christ (the mystics have a category for this, called 'discursive meditation'): 'for this is not the time for it'. Rather, we should go so far as to desire this loss of our own ideas to happen quickly, so we may receive

> the contemplation that God is bestowing ... and make room in [our] spirits for the enkindling and burning of the love that this dark and

> secret contemplation bears and communicates to the soul. For contemplation is nothing else than a secret and peaceful and loving inflow of God, which, if not hampered, fires the soul in the spirit of love.[82]

This is the reason that John wrote in the next line that he was – and we can be – 'fired with love's urgent longings'. We move on now to find out how this works.

In the darkness, it is a great gift if we can understand that it is our longing for Love that is calling us. This overwhelming longing for wholeness is in a way the cause of our pain. But it is in fact a gift. If we had no sense of love and did not feel it was our destiny to experience it, we would not feel so lost when it disappears.

> At times with this condition, a person will feel a certain longing for God. The fire increases and the soul becomes aware of being attracted in the love of God and being enkindled in it ... the longings for God become so intense that it will seem to people their bones are drying up in this thirst, their nature withering away.[83]

The suffering and loss experienced by people in the darkness feels like a withering away, certainly. But the insight John gives is that in reality this is a longing for the Other, for God, for the Author of Love, the Divine Lover. It is a longing for an end to alienation and to experience the embrace of our maker, but it comes in the depths of darkness.

John says:

> The soul that receives this must suffer greatly ... When the rays of pure light strike upon the soul to expel its impurities, the soul perceives itself to so unclean and miserable ... it thinks that God has abandoned it ... The second way in which the soul suffers pain comes from natural moral and spiritual weakness ... It is under an immense and dark burden – suffering and groaning in agony so great that the soul would consider death a relief.[84]

John's great insight is to say: 'This dark night is an inflowing of God into the soul which cleanses it of its ignorance and imperfections, habitual, natural and spiritual.' Contemplatives call this 'infused contemplation', meaning contemplation that brings into us, or like healing herbal tea, to use a banal image, infuses us with the very power and presence of God. He says: 'God secretly searches the soul and instructs it in the perfection of love ... This affects the soul in two ways: it purifies and it enlightens. Thus, in the end, 'contemplation prepares the soul for union with God in love.'[85]

So it is that he calls it 'grace' ('Ah! the sheer grace'). He believes that: 'The endurance of darkness is the preparation for great light.' It is a position of faith.

– Ah! the sheer grace! –
I went out unseen, my house being now all stilled.[86]

This is a time of poverty, of weakness, of not knowing how to proceed with life in the way we used to. And this is the point: for the person seeking God and seeking Love, John says that now is the time to do things completely differently – and this brings hope. He explains:

Poor, abandoned and unsupported (in the darkness of my intellect, the distress of my will and in the affliction and anguish of my memory), left to darkness in pure faith ... and my will touched by the sorrows, afflictions and longings of love of God, I went out from myself. That is, I departed from my low manner of understanding and my feeble way of loving.[87]

John wants us to 'go out of ourselves': to leave old ways – perhaps old armour or self-protective habits are to be discarded – so that in terms of experiencing God's presence, we can leave ourselves and enter into God. Now that 'our house is stilled', we can gaze on and lean on God in a new way – maybe for the first time.

Dear spiritual friend, if you feel this aloneness and darkness; If you feel at the end of your understanding – and in the grip of despair and loss – Hold on! And reach out ... Help is on the way.

The first verse ends: 'My house being now all stilled.' John felt that the way through is found in stillness and quiet. He says: 'It is great wisdom to know how to be silent and to look at neither the remarks, nor the deeds, nor the lives of others.'

In our darkness the great and addictive temptation is to turn to words, media, messages from others, diverting clips. But in the end these do little but distract us briefly.

Blaise Pascal, seventeenth-century mathematician and mystic, was one of the first, in his *Pensées*, to name this as a trap leading to death:

> The only thing that consoles us for our miseries is 'distractions'. And yet this is the greatest of our miseries. For it is this above all which prevents us thinking about ourselves and leads us imperceptibly to destruction. But for that we would be bored, and boredom would drive us to seek more solid means of escape, but distraction passes our time and leads us imperceptibly to death.[88]

Since then, this idea has been popularized in books like *Amusing Ourselves to Death* and *Distracting Ourselves to Death*.[89]

But for the Dark Night journey of mystics, it is in fact the countercultural silence that will bring us peace with God. Silence becomes a form of mindfulness therapy, but with the Beloved present in the room and the author of peace and also as our longed-for destination. Thus it is not in fact impossible to achieve.

Mystical practice calls us to leave our old ways of distraction behind radically and completely, to be attentive. To abide in God. As we go 'out of ourselves', as John puts it, we can experience joy and light can flood into the darkness. John says:

> This was a great happiness for me, because through the annihilation and calming of my faculties, passion, appetites, and affections, I went out from my human operation and way of acting, to God's operation and way of acting – that is my Intellect departed from itself, changing from human and natural to divine – to be united with God … And my Will departed from itself, and became divine, united with the divine love. It no longer lives in a lowly manner with its natural strength, but with the strength and purity of the Holy Spirit. And finally, all the strength and affections of the soul by means of this night and purgation of the old man are renewed with divine qualities and delights.[90]

'The Dark Night of the Soul' continues and describes just this renewal and union:

> O guiding night!
> O night more lovely than the dawn!
> O night that has united
> The Lover with his beloved,
> Transforming the beloved in her Lover.[91]

The Apostle Paul writes of this possibility of union and of transformation. He tells the Galatians of his own experience of the dark night: 'I have been crucified with Christ and I no longer live, but Christ in me' (Gal. 2.10). This is the step-change: and it is for John and many mystics unobtainable without some kind of dark night of the soul.

The journey, after the night or within the night, brings Union. Elsewhere, in his comments on 'The Spiritual Canticle', John speaks of the soul's progression to Union and Communion:

> When the soul has lived for some time as the betrothed of the Son of God, in perfect and sweet love, God calls her into his flowering garden ... Then the two natures are so united. What is divine is so communicated to what is human that without undergoing any essential change, each seems to be of God.[92]

John adds: 'Yet in this life the union cannot be perfect ... and cannot be described or conceived.'

John's friend St Teresa of Avila agrees:

> One who has had experience of this will understand it in some measure: but it cannot be more clearly described because what takes place is so obscure. All you are able to say is, that the soul is represented as being close to God, and that there abides a conviction so certain and strong that it cannot possibly help believing it so.[93]

Teresa and John are lost for words. But if this Union with God cannot be described, how can we tell of it?

One solution found in the Bible – and ever since – is that we turn to poetry: union with God is described primarily in the great poem at the heart of the Bible, The Song of Songs, John's great Bible text that he was constantly expounding. Perhaps this is one reason why all of John's great writings are in the form of poetry. He cannot describe his mystical journey other than in poetry, which, like good art, 'compresses the coal of truth into diamonds'.[94]

Evelyn Underhill wrote:

> The artist is no more and no less than a contemplative who has learned to express themselves and who tells of their love in colour, speech, or sound. The mystic is an artist of a special and exalted kind who tries to express something of the revelation they have received.[95]

She makes much of the closeness of the mystic to the artist – the poet – mainly because the poet, the painter, the composer at their best get *inside and become one with* their apprehension of Reality (she writes it with a capital 'R'). She says we all experience the mystical when

> some great emotion, some devastating visitation of beauty, love or pain lifts us to another level of consciousness, and we are aware for a moment of the difference between the neat collection of objects and experiences we call 'the world' – and the height, the length, the breadth of that living, growing, changing Fact in which we live and move and have our being. When this happens, 'sensation' is freed from the tyranny of what we call 'thought'.[96]

We will return to this theme of creativity as one way to navigate our path through the Dark Night.

> O night that has united
> The Lover with his Beloved,[97]

The goal or result of the Dark Night is the mystery of Union with God (uniting the Lover with his beloved). And this is what the poet of the Song of Songs expressed two thousand years earlier. In the Song we read the Bride saying at last, after a night of darkness and loss: 'Let my beloved come into my garden and taste its choicest fruits.' To which the Bridegroom replies: 'I have come into my garden, my sister, my bride. I have gathered my myrrh with my aromatic spices' (Song 5.1).

John concludes: 'And now that the soul lives, a life, so happy, and so glorious ... consider what a sweet life it must be a – life, where God sees nothing that is displeasing, and now the soul finds nothing irksome, but rather the glory and the light of God.'[98]

But before this there is darkness. Fiction writers put it powerfully: Koestler's *Darkness at Noon*, Conrad's *Heart of Darkness*, Asimov's *Nightfall*. We pause now to address the black, dark night pervading our culture. Hopefully we will find a way through it.

© Peronel Barnes, Saatbrak

Peronel succeeds in showing the beauty of the Night against contrasting brightness. Sometimes when a person goes through darkness there can come a refining and a beauty of character – a meekness that emerges too, if we would but see it in the background luminous night.

3

Our Culture's Dark Night of the Soul

> Where have You hidden Yourself,
> And abandoned me in my groaning, O my Beloved?
> You have fled like the hart,
> Having wounded me.
> I ran after You, crying; but You were gone ...
> Oh who can heal me?
> Give me at once Yourself,
> Send me no more
> A messenger
> Who cannot tell me what I wish.
> All they who serve are telling me
> Of Your unnumbered graces;
> And all wound me more and more,
> And something leaves me dying
> ('The Spiritual Canticle')[99]

John of the Cross's great poem 'The Spiritual Canticle' describes the sense of angst and woundedness that are the experience of so many people today: 'Where have you hidden yourself and abandoned me in my groaning?' Of people trying to comfort him he says: 'All wound me more and more and something leaves me dying.'

It is my conviction that this absence of meaning, hope, even love is not only experienced by those seeking God but also by those who have turned away from him. The absence of God was what was deeply felt by twentieth-century philosophers who in the end rejected God. They were 'Waiting for Godot' – but God never came to them. As John says above: 'Where have you hidden Yourself and abandoned me in your groaning, O my Beloved?'

Already in 1889, Nietsche prophetically baptized the twentieth century as an age of 'The Twilight of the Gods', lamenting over their loss but hammering them out of view. I would suggest that this experience of the absence of God led an existentialist like Sartre to write his book *Being and Nothingness*. *The Outsider* (*L'étranger*) is the name given in Albert Camus' novel to this sense of the alienation of a generation. Camus wrote his novel *The Plague*, now viewed as prophetic, about responses during a random pandemic. The response of faith in God seems absurd in an environment without meaning. I believe these writers have defined our age. Their thinking still dominates popular absurdist online and TV platforms today. These forums don't hesitate to ignore or even ridicule God, who seems irrelevant in a now post-modern twenty-first-century world.[100]

I believe this ghosting of God – sidelining and then maybe ignoring him – often comes from a place of pain and darkness, albeit anaesthetized with humour. Questions of meaning may be drowned out by the noise of chattering life needing to be occupied 24/7, but the existentialists' perennial question remains: How do we find meaning?

The existentialists made a 'courageous virtue' out of the absence of God and created a Brave New World without him, but one can sometimes sense the sadness and regret in their writing. It became a Dark Night for many of them. They echo John of the Cross, whose Spiritual Canticle says: 'Having wounded me. I ran after You, crying; but You were gone'.

Novelist Julian Barnes once said: 'I don't believe in God – but I miss him.' Sartre wrote: 'that God is dead, I cannot deny. That my whole being cries out for God, I can never forget.' He said in his autobiography *Words* (*Les Mots*):

> I had more difficulty getting rid of the Holy Spirit in that he had installed himself in the basement of my mind. I collared him and threw him out ... Atheism is a long hard business. I believe I am now like a man who no longer has any reason for living.[101]

Their German contemporary Bertolt Brecht flirted with communism before finding that it too led to ashes. His work is steeped in Bible references and language, but always used with mocking irony. These writers were arguably always aware of God, or rather of his absence.[102] Albert Camus wanted to have it both ways, saying: 'I do not believe in God and I am not an atheist.'[103] He then addressed head on the question of whether or not the authentic thing to do when faced with the perceived meaninglessness of our existence is to kill ourselves. He became the contemporary of so many people today amid the threat of suicide among young and anxious people.

John of the Cross writes: 'And all people wound me more and more, And something leaves me dying.'

Dying is an experience of the Dark Night that was part of the journey of mystics like John. It is also one of the central questions of Camus' *The Myth of Sisyphus* (1942), which concludes that suicide is an inadequate solution to our existential dilemma and that, instead, we should rebel through a clear-sighted and relentless describing of our perceived futile condition. Camus explores the apparent meaninglessness of the universe, our confrontation with this hopelessness and the potential solutions to this intolerable condition (which, he suggests, might include suicide). He uses the image of Sisyphus constantly pushing a huge boulder up a mountain only to have it, in an absurd universe, roll down to the bottom each time he arrives at the top. He wrote: 'Should I kill myself, or have a cup of coffee? … But in the end, one needs more courage to live than to kill himself.' Camus is paradoxical in that he wrote: 'In the midst of winter, I found there was, within me, an invincible summer.'[104]

These and other thinkers are important to note because they formalized the fact that ours is a 'post Christian era' in the West. Of course, some find a way to live hopefully and even fruitfully despite the absence of God. But at the same time, in my view, the pervasive cultural climate of the absence of God, and the absence of hope in him and subsequent pessimism concerning life beyond death and the hope of heaven, greatly increase the frequency and severity of the experience of the Dark Night today.

Europe today is also turning away to the darkness of life without God, if we watch carefully. It is said that while it took 500 years for our continent to become a largely Christian continent, it has only taken fifty years for that worldview in so many places to be airbrushed away – though thankfully the roots and the wells remain. When living in the heart of Oxford for nearly 20 years, we witnessed one of many transformations of our revered medieval city's heart – like heart bypass surgery – as a new shopping centre was built. For two years the huge project's building work was hidden behind colourful hoardings proudly telling 'the Story of Oxford'. Space was allotted to the University's free-thinking origins, battles fought between 'Town and Gown', Oxford's prison, the University's different inventions such as penicillin, and the city's such as the Morris Minor and then the Mini. Famous Oxford names were mentioned like Hobbes, Halley, Samuel Johnson, Einstein, Stephen Hawking, Oscar Wilde and Richard Dawkins among others.

What was completely omitted, presumably as something 'people would not be interested in', was the fact that the University's origins were Christian, with her patron saint St Frideswide's eighth-century abbey and the brilliant Franciscans who settled here in the thirteenth century. Erased was her Christian motto 'Dominus Illuminatio Mea' (Psalm 27), and the fact that nearly all her colleges are Christian foundations with Christian names (Christ Church, St John's, Jesus College, Trinity, St Catherine's, St Anne's St Hugh's, Magdalen and so on). The fact that Bishops Latimer Ridley and Cranmer were martyred for their faith at the heart of Oxford was apparently no longer part of the 'Story of Oxford'. Omitted completely was Oxford being the cradle of the eighteenth-century nation-changing revival, with John Wesley a faculty member and George Whitfield finding faith here. Nor did we hear tell of the Oxford movement or of Oxfam. Oxford's 'history' did not apparently include the fact that C. S. Lewis and J. R. R. Tolkien wrote their brilliant Christian novels here. For this was the city of atheist authors like Dawkins, Christopher Hitchens and Philip Pullman – and this is the post-Christian world.

For me, this is part of the background to our Dark Night condition. Perhaps the present darkness is receding: I hope so. A recent publication charts the reaction of several academics, mainly scientists, to the so-called 'new atheism'. It tells of their sometimes mystical or often logical journeys towards the Christian faith. The book is intriguingly titled *Finding Faith through Dawkins*.[105]

But in my view still, so often the popular, philosophical zeitgeist has been darkness all around. We live in a world of loss. And we are now living through yet more destruction: a new seemingly endless European war and even the unthinkable threat of nuclear conflict is with us. In addition, more conflict for the nations of the Holy Land, with the risk of missiles setting an entire region on fire. And as a backdrop, there is a crisis for our whole planet's climate, bringing extreme weather never experienced before.

How do we navigate this Dark Night? What language can we find?

4

Ways through the Darkness: Healing Creativity

We need to remember that we are created creative …
(Maya Angelou, *Wouldn't Take Nothing for My Journey Now*)[106]

To be human is to be creative.
(Makoto Fujimura, *Art and Faith*)[107]

One way in which the existentialists and their contemporary successors responded to darkness was, remarkably, to create unforgettable, jewel-like works of art. These are forged in the darkness.

The fact is, Camus and others found some salvation in the very act of creating. Camus' writing is of extreme, haunting beauty. As he famously said: 'Live to the point of tears.' He is a poet who holds on to life by his fingertips. John of the Cross is a poet who by contrast held on to *God* by his fingertips. In *The Ascent of Mount Carmel* he describes 'the darknesses and trials spiritual and temporal that fortunate souls ordinarily undergo on their way … so numerous and profound that human science cannot understand them adequately'. He says: 'experience of them does not equip one to explain them'. So it is that he resorts to poetry. He subtitles 'The Dark Night of the Soul': 'A song of the soul's happiness in having passed through the dark night of faith, in nakedness and purgation, to union with the Beloved'.[108]

So in the end it is a creative's song. Creativity is one path to help us through the darkness. It is one palliative medicine we can take in the Dark Night. It is available to all, it is within all of our grasps. We will mention others in the pages to come, but for now my conviction is that creativity is a gift to every person, for we are made in the image of God. The Divine Artist has made us and part of being whole and human is liberating creativity. There is therapeutic healing in growing into and discovering how to create and have some artistic expression in its broadest sense in our lives.

We may respond: 'I'm not like that. I'm not poetic, I can't or don't paint and I'm not a musician.' But the fact is: you *are* creative. I believe everyone, without exception, has what Jung calls 'an instinct for Creativity'.[109] Society romanticizes 'creators', often to the point of indulgence. But I'm not talking about that. I'm talking about a broad scope that includes writing, music, painting, homemaking, design, garden creativity. I include creativity at work, building friendship communities, creativity in family, in sport and in lifestyle, online creativity and much more – so, a broad definition. Whatever it is, creativity can be born even in the darkness, or coming out of darkness. And one way through the Dark Night is to recover creativity. Try writing, try painting (however dark you may paint), recover creativity. Cook, sing, join a choir or a team. I don't underestimate the effort and risk, especially if there is depression lurking on the horizon. I don't speak lightly. But maybe turn sorrow into shadows in a painting. Transform weariness into words. Develop dark negatives into sharp images of truth.

As psychologist Thomas Moore says: 'A creative person participates in the Creator's work. The creation of the world is an ongoing project and part of the divinity of the human being – an idea cherished by Renaissance philosophers – is to add to that process.'[110] This is why the Dark Night can be illumined a little by creativity: it is healing medicine. The quiet act of creating can be like restorative mindfulness. It repairs. Indeed, Anne Holmes writes: 'I believe that Creative Repair is an essential practice for anyone involved in helping others. This includes those in parenting roles who often need permission to take time out for themselves.' *Creative Repair* is the title of her helpful book which examines how this works.[111]

During one lockdown, I spent time online doing some watercolour painting with one of my grandchildren. The act of preparing materials, discussing and then being absorbed inside an image, 'seeing' it, then drawing and painting together did us good. Even (perhaps especially?) the mutual 'active silence' was healing.

I have mentioned Evelyn Underhill already. She was a writer and poet who experienced a spiritual conversion in 1907 and began studying the lives of the mystics. She turned her upstairs study in the home she shared with her husband into a frequently used prayer room, where she wrote and prayed each day. She came to prominence with her insightful and thorough *Mysticism* (1911), a classic on the subject. She writes:

the life of pure sensation is the meat and drink of poetry and this is one of the most accessible avenues to that union with Reality which the mystic says is the very point of Life ... I include in the sweep of poetic art the coloured poetry of the painter, the wordless poetry of the musician and the dancer too.[112]

Underhill goes further, saying: 'Contemplation is ... the essential activity of all artists. By it they may achieve that heavenly power of communion with the veritable life ... freed from the tyranny of that which we call "thought".'[113] So it is that we move from contemplating the natural world – or indeed the built world – to becoming one with it. The mystic becomes the artist who tries to express something of the revelation he or she has received; the artist is a contemplative who has learned to express herself.

Poetry and the act of Creation as a means to describe and journey through the Dark Night are among John of the Cross's great discoveries. In the Bible, too, coping with darkness is expressed in poetry. John's poetry follows in a grand tradition. We find that around one-third of the poems of the book of Psalms deal with disorientation and sadness – they describe the Dark Night. Psalm 55.4 is one example:

> My heart is in anguish within me;
>   the terrors of death have fallen upon me.
> Fear and trembling have beset me,
>   horror has overwhelmed me.

Psalm 102.3–4 is another:

> For my days vanish like smoke;
>   my bones burn like glowing embers.
> My heart is blighted and withered like grass;
>   I forget to eat my bread.

Some of the most compelling language of darkness in the whole world's literature is found in the Bible, in Jeremiah's Lamentations. This was written in the context of one of the most traumatic moments in the whole of the Old Testament – the fall of Jerusalem. Massive human suffering at every level – physical and emotional – ensued, and the humiliation of the small nation of Israel: the disappearance of the monarchy, the priesthood, the temple and 'ichabod' – the departure of the glory of God. All this was gone.

As I have said, Europe is not without similar loss today, if we dare to care.

In Jeremiah's day, the trauma and pain gave birth to poetry: the Book of Lamentations – 'daring to describe the indescribable and utter the unutterable – and to do so in poetry of astonishing beauty and intricacy, though soaked in tears'.[114] Lamentations was written to give language to darkness. I believe that to acknowledge sadness and pain and loss is a sign of emotional reality and health. One way to express this may be through creativity.

In my own life I have known times of loss, bereavement, separation and sadness. But my own experience, at first, was to walk through them without any idea of how to cope with darkness other than in an unhealthy way. I did not learn lament or any expression when my parents divorced when I was 14 years old. I did not really learn this when our first son died in a cot death seven years after our marriage. I failed to embrace it many years later when a beloved member of our family contracted cancer and began a long, sad struggle with sickness ending in their death. It was not until later, when a friend, an exceptional 36-year-old woman on our team, much loved by all, was run over by a cement lorry and killed on her way to work, that I learnt – and we learnt as a community – to grieve. We began to learn a new language, that of Lament, and entered a period of healing as a result. I wish I'd learnt it sooner. It was a big price to pay. Then this lamenting flowed back into all these other stories.

The Bible's Dark Night poem called 'Lamentations' is a five-chapter book with a brilliant structure. Each of the first four chapters is an acrostic, with each verse beginning with the next letter of the 22-letter Hebrew alphabet. This structure (not visible in English translations) gives some order to the utter chaos of what is being described. Like a trellis up which a wild rose with sharp thorns and delicate fragrance is trained, so the anarchic words are woven and pinned into this scaffold of life-giving structure. People's terrible conditions are listed with their pain and suffering in these famous lines:

> How deserted lies the city,
>   once so full of people!
> How like a widow is she,
>   who once was great among the nations!
> She who was queen among the provinces
>   has now become a slave.

Bitterly she weeps at night,
   tears are on her cheeks ...
All her friends have betrayed her;
   they have become her enemies ...
The roads to Zion mourn.
(Lam. 1, vv. 1, 2 and 4)

'All her friends have betrayed her' is a contemporary dark night feeling that people express. What are we to do?

Sometimes when teaching on this subject, I have introduced the following exercise and I do so now in the hope that it may be helpful and bring creative light in the darkness. I've encouraged people to write their own lament about a situation they have faced, using the structure of the 26 letters of the English alphabet. Thus:

Agony has fallen on me
Broken hearted because of loss and loneliness
Cries in the dark night do not console
Desert and dread are the landscapes in my soul ...

And so on. I believe that poetic structure – in this case the alphabet as in the book of Lamentations – used as a trellis for words of pain and abandonment and the Dark Night, can help us through. As John created poetry and the existentialists survived through their finely-chiselled words, so we may find help here too.

Claude Monet's 'The Water Lilies' was produced during the intensity of the violent trauma of the First World War, part of a vast series that he called his 'monument to peace'.[115] In his anguish about the destruction of the war, Monet did the only thing that he felt he could do in response to pain on such a vast scale: he painted. We may not paint with the majesty of Monet. But even the plethora of mindful colouring books are not completely removed from this healing gift of creativity – and everything artistic in-between; even the piecing together of a puzzle can be symbolic and creative therapy. Try painting the darkness. Van Gogh, who lived through his own dark night, wrote to his brother: 'One of the most beautiful things to do is to paint darkness, which nevertheless has light in it.' John of the Cross's mystical poems are really word-paintings.

Dear spiritual friend, how might this happen in your own life journey to wholeness? If you don't do so already, might you adopt habits of living that include creativity as a weekly or frequent mystical discipline?

Writing a rule of life with priorities for ourselves has become popular again. But often these rules of life confine themselves to prayer rhythms or aspirations. For myself, I feel our rule of life can be broader, more balanced, healing and godly for us when stretched to include family, hospitality, building friendships, time in Creation but also Creativity and creative repair. The mystics lead us to this as a way through the darkness of the days we are called to inhabit.

When the time came for the Tabernacle to be built for God's presence in the wilderness, Moses was told about God's love for creativity:

> See I have chosen Bezalel – I have filled him with the Spirit ... to devise artistic designs to work in gold, silver and bronze and their setting – carving wood, to work in every craft. And I have chosen Oholiab ... and I have given to all able people ability to create ... (Ex. 31.1–7)

They are the first biblical artists, thus showing the Creator's seal of the Holy Spirit on people who are creatives. Pete Greig, an influencer who leads a community of 24/7 prayer and whose core values include creativity, writes: 'Whether or not I consider myself as having any particular skills as an artist, what creative abilities has God given me that I might use to help make a dwelling place for his presence?'[116]

One mystic particularly coming into focus today as one of the prominent women leaders in the medieval church is Hildegard of Bingen.

Hildegard was born around 1098. She was a writer, composer, philosopher, mystic and visionary who went on to found several convents and monasteries. From early childhood, her spiritual awareness was grounded in what she called the 'reflection of the living Light'. She describes her experience in a letter:

> From my early childhood ... I have always seen this vision in my soul, even to the present time when I am more than seventy years old. In this vision, my soul, as God would have it, rises up high into the vault of heaven and into the changing sky and spreads itself out among different peoples, although they are far away from me in distant lands and places. And because I see them this way in my soul, I observe them in accord with the shifting of clouds and other created things. I do not hear them with my outward ears, nor do I perceive them by the thoughts of my own heart or by any combination of my five senses, but in my soul alone, while my outward eyes are open. ... I call it 'the reflection of the living Light'. And as the sun, the moon, and the

stars appear in water, so writings, sermons, virtues, and certain human actions take form for me and gleam.[117]

Hildegard is the patron saint of artists, being herself a talented poet and musician. She writes: 'The Word is living, being, spirit, all verdant greening, all creativity. This Word manifests itself in every creature.' The Word is 'all creativity'. Her writings are exactly this: creative and imaginative. She writes of God:

> I am the fiery life of the essence of God; I am the flame above the beauty in the fields; I shine in the waters; I burn in the sun, the moon, and the stars. And with the airy wind, I quicken all things vitally by an unseen, all-sustaining life.

To each of us she gives this charge, in words that could refer to the calling to create:

> Dare to declare who you are. It is not far from the shores of silence to the boundaries of speech. The path is not long, but the way is deep. You must not only walk there, you must be prepared to leap.[118]

5

Ways through the Darkness: Healing Nature

My Beloved is in the mountains,
The solitary wooded valleys,
The strange islands,
The roaring torrents,
The whisper of the amorous gales;
The tranquil night
At the approaches of the dawn,
The silent music,
The murmuring solitude,
The supper which revives, and enkindles love. ...
Light-winged birds,
Lions, fawns, bounding does,
Mountains, valleys, strands,
Waters, winds, heat,
And the terrors that keep watch by night.
(John of the Cross, 'The Spiritual Canticle')[119]

Henry Thoreau is famous for the line 'Most people live lives of quiet desperation.' The full sentence reads: 'Most people lead lives of quiet desperation – what is called resignation is confirmed desperation. From the desperate city, you go to the desperate country, and have to console yourself with the bravery of minks and muskrats.' What in fact he was calling for, long before this became fashionable, was that healing can be found in nature. He said: 'I went to the woods because I wished to live deliberately – and see if I could learn what it had to teach and not, when I came to die, discover that I had not lived.'[120]

As well as creativity, another pathway through the Dark Night of the Soul is to be immersed, drenched, bathed in creation. This is something that John of the Cross longed for, it seems.

His only view of it during those nine dark months in prison was of the sky through his barred prison window. But he frequently brings the beauty of the created world to us through his writing. In his 'Spiritual Canticle' quoted above, he speaks of travelling through the 'solitary wooded valleys, strange islands, the roaring torrents, the whisper of winds' that he calls amorous. This is immersion in nature and extolling its beauties as a love affair. Then he summons up the calm before the dawn: the paradox of 'silent music': it is as if we strain our ears to hear it – and we can! The solitude 'murmuring' as it does, inviting him to the 'supper that revives' – a reference to the Eucharist – a looking forward to the book of Revelation's 'Blessed are they who are invited to the wedding supper of the Lamb' (Rev. 19.9).

Then immediately we are creation bathing again: 'birds, lions, fawns, does … and mountains, valleys, beaches, waters, winds, heat'. John is glorying in God's rich creation teeming with life in all its fullness. Some feel that we are 'born nature mystics'. It is true that infants are charmed with bright colours, and as children we discover the secret world of cloud formations and sounds. As we grow in our appreciation we are in awe of sunrises and sunsets. We instinctively turn to the beauty of our world. In it, it may be that we discover the thing for which our senses were made, our common bond with nature: 'And God saw that it was good.'[121]

John ends the verse by evoking 'the terrors that keep watch by night'. This is a reminder of the nearness of ecstasy to agony, the proximity of Glory and Fear. John's dark night imprisonment was a terror, as was the threat of spiritual darkness. This phrase is a reference to Song of Songs 3.8. Chapter 3 is one of two sections about the Night and Darkness in the Song. It begins, 'All night long on my bed I looked for the one my heart loves; I looked for him but did not find him.'

It ends with the finding of the Beloved and seeing his carriage surrounded by sixty warriors 'all armed against the terrors of the night'. Here, John of the Cross's language is ambivalent, and we don't know whether he is speaking about protection against the terrors or the terrors in creation themselves. And no doubt both count: there is protection and safety – but also Awe and Fear in the Presence.

John of the Cross became the Spiritual Mentor of his friend Teresa of Avila, who herself founded several communities attempting to follow Christ more closely. They were both part of the Carmelite order, which gathered many followers of Christ into community at that time. They take their name from the Carmel mountain range where Elijah's courageous stand against the prophets of Baal took place. They also remember Elijah's encounter with God in the hiding place in the rock after his flight to Mount Sinai. This is a creation scene which influenced a whole movement: Elijah, the first Carmelite, saw the Earthquake, the Rushing Wind, the Fire. But it was in the Silence – the still small voice – that he met God after the fire. Elijah's therapy was found in this cave, in being alone, being in creation and being quiet. And ours can be too. For 'in the day of trouble he shall hide me in his shelter; in the secret place of his dwelling shall he hide me and set me high upon a rock' (Psalm 27).

When darkness strikes, one great therapy is to be alone and quiet in nature, letting creation surround us if we can. As John said:

> It is best to learn to silence the faculties and to cause them to be still so that God may speak ... What we need most in order to make progress is to be silent before this great God with our appetite and with our tongue, for the language he best hears is silent love.[122]

Dear spiritual friend, do you consciously exit 'the racket' to enter golden nature?

Gerard Manley Hopkins (1844–89) was a Jesuit priest and also a mystic capable of seeing God's beauty in creation and presence within it, and then expressing this with great power and beauty. In 'God's Grandeur' he describes creation as being packed with the glory of its Author:

> The world is charged with the grandeur of God.
>   It will flame out, like shining from shook foil;
>   It gathers to a greatness, like the ooze of oil
> Crushed.[123]

Hopkins finds that despite creation being so exploited and neglected by humans who have blundered through it, the fact is:

> For all this, nature is never spent;
>   There lives the dearest freshness deep down things; ...
>   Because the Holy Ghost over the bent
>   World broods with warm breast and with ah! bright wings.[124]

For Hopkins, the reason nature is never worn out or spent is because 'The Holy Ghost over the bent world broods.'[125]

Maybe this brooding of the Holy Spirit is why, in fact, the natural world of creation heals people, and doctors now prescribe spending time in contact with the natural world as therapeutic. The term 'forest bathing' appears. And in fact this total immersion is an accurate description of what mystics experience.

In our day this is prescribed like medication as a way to combat stress and improve health. Studies focusing on exercising in nature have found improvements in self-esteem, particularly among the young.[126] Unsurprisingly, overall effects on mood were heightened when there was a stream or other body of water nearby. Although mechanisms to explain technically how all this happens still evade scientists, many researchers and health professionals do believe that contact with nature improves and maintains one's health. Of course, the Bible speaks of the positive effects of contact with creation. David's 'still waters', beside which God restored his soul even as he entered the dark valley of the shadow of death (Psalm 23.1–3) are worth finding! He was moved mentally and spiritually to rejoice and meditate when he gazed on the grandeur of all God has created (Psalm 104). When he realized how small he was in the vastness of God's creation, David was comforted to know that God was mindful of him (Psalm 8.1–6).

Hopkins compares humans to kingfishers who, as they 'catch fire', cry, 'What I do is me: for that I came!' He goes on to say that when man exercises justice with Grace, it is in fact because each day 'Christ plays in a thousand places'.

> The just man justices;
> Keeps grace: thát keeps all his goings graces;
> Acts in God's eye what in God's eye he is –
> Chríst – for Christ plays in ten thousand places,
> Lovely in limbs, and lovely in eyes not his
> To the Father through the features of men's faces.[127]

'Christ plays in ten thousand places ... through the features of men's faces.' This is so hopeful a view that when immersed in creation it can flood us with joy, if only we will let it.

However, it has to be said that to be present in silence in creation is just as challenging as being present when alone in one's room. A 'discipline of attentiveness' is needed here too. Many, when out walking or running, never hear the sound of creation – let alone the sound of silence – because of neglect, or because of their headphones or earbuds and the perpetual noise of music or podcasts or phone-calls. Even in nature, it remains a radical choice to *see*. Hildegard of Bingen writes (my italics):

> *Glance* at the sun. *See* the moon and the stars. *Gaze* at the beauty of the Earth's greenings. Now, think.

What are we to think of? She continues:

> There is the music of Heaven in all things ... Every creature is a glistening, glittering mirror of divinity.

Evelyn Underhill had the same conviction around a thousand years later. She tells the old story of 'Eyes' and 'No-Eyes' as the story of mystical and non-mystical capacity:

> 'No-Eyes' has fixed his attention on the fact that he is obliged to take a walk. For him, the chief factor of existence is movement along the road, a movement which he intends to accomplish as comfortably as he can. He asks not to know what might be on either side of the hedges. He ignores the caress of the wind until it threatens to remove his hat. He trudges along steadily, diligently avoiding the muddy puddles while oblivious of the light which they reflect.
>
> 'Eyes' takes the walk too. For him, it is a perpetual revelation of beauty and wonder; the sunlight inebriates him, the winds delight him and the very effort of the journey is a joy. Magic presences throng the roadside or cry greetings to him from the hidden fields. The rich world through which he moves lies in the foreground of his consciousness and gives up new secrets at every step.
>
> 'No-Eyes', when told of these adventures usually refuses to believe that both have gone along the same road. He thinks that his companion has been floating about in the air or having agreeable hallucinations.[128]

Underhill concludes tellingly: 'We shall never persuade him to the contrary, unless we persuade him to look for himself, therefore, it's to a practical mysticism that the practical person is here invited.'[129]

It takes a poet (as so often) to help us to see the beauty, including the beauty of the Darkness. In *The Vast Night*, twentieth-century German mystical poet Rainer Maria Rilke stands before the night and its darkness and bathes in it as eventually, he says, its 'smile enters my heart':

> Often I stood at the window begun the day before,
> stood and gazed at you in wonder ...
> I stand and suddenly understand that you
> Deep Night, you play with me
> And I gaze at you in wonder ...[130]

Today, many seek solace in shopping centres, cinemas and, sweating in gyms, watch exercise videos; many are housed in urban high-rise apartment buildings, living life online, cut off from the natural world. This separation can be a dark night. For those seeking solace from God, being in nature can heal and help.

Dear spiritual friend, we have seen that for John of the Cross there was a yearning for creation even in his dark prison cell. For ourselves, finding the energy to be in Creation is a pathway through the Darkness.

Here is another poet theologian Wendell Berry. His 'The Peace of Wild Things' is as good a summary for this chapter as I can find:

> When despair for the world grows in me,
> and I wake in the night at the least sound
> in fear of what my life and my children's lives may be,
> I go and lie down where the wood drake
> rests in his beauty on the water, and the great heron feeds.
> I come into the peace of wild things
> who do not tax their lives with the forethought
> of grief. I come into the presence of still water.
> And I feel above me the day-blind stars
> waiting with their light. For a time
> I rest in the grace of the world, and am free.[131]

6

Ways through the Darkness: Spiritual Friendships

Friends:
How is your beloved better than others,
most beautiful of women?
How is your beloved better than others,
that you so charge us?
She:
My beloved is ...
   outstanding among ten thousand.
(Song 5.9–10)

Friends:
Where has your beloved gone,
   most beautiful of women?
Which way did your beloved turn,
   that we may look for him with you?
She:
My beloved has gone down to his garden,
   to the beds of spices ...
I am my beloved's and my beloved is mine;
   he browses among the lilies.
(Song 6.1–3)

We may think that the mystical journey is essentially a lonely pathway of solitude and silence away from people. But this is to misunderstand the experience of deep, spiritual friendship that mystics also enjoy and call us to.

Most medieval mystics found their inspiration in the Bible's Song of Songs, where old traditions give us repeated, mysterious references to the Bride's 'friends', who encourage her at different times. In Song of Songs 5.9 they encourage the Bride to speak about her Beloved, saying:

> How is your beloved better than others,
>   most beautiful of women?
> How is your beloved better than others,
>   that you so charge us?

She replies that he is 'outstanding among ten thousand'. In the search for the Beloved, in Songs 6, quoted above, they tell the Bride that they want to 'look for him with her'. They encourage the Bride to express her affection. They will help her find the Beloved who is lost from her sight.

The fact is that this is exactly similar to the role the mystics played for one another in their spiritual direction and spiritual friendship relationships. I believe that it was spiritual friendships that took them through the dark night that they experienced – and that will take us through it too, if we find such friends and cultivate such friendships. Of course, at the darkest night of all, Jesus himself looked to his deep friendships among the twelve, but particularly among the three: Peter, James, and John the beloved disciple who lay his head near Jesus' heart at the last supper.

Famous spiritual friendships are seen between John of the Cross and Teresa of Avila. In a similar way, Francis de Sales and Jane de Chantal forged deep friendship in the 1600s in France. The same was true of Francis of Assisi and Clare and of many others. This gift of friendship is a very present help in time of trouble in the dark night, as it can be today. 'There is nothing on earth more to be prized than true friendship' said Aquinas.

John of the Cross was a close friend to his 'Directee' St Teresa of Avila. She teasingly called him 'half a friar' because of his small height. They were great friends: she was animated, witty and chatty; he was more reserved, gentle and unnoticed.

It was Teresa who recruited John to the cause of reforming the Carmelite order. If ever there was a saint who dispels the notion that the universal call to holiness means becoming bleak and colourless, it was St Teresa of Avila.

Born in 1515 at or near Avila, Spain, she is a Doctor of the Catholic Church. She became a reformer of the Carmelite order and an author of spiritual classics such as *The Way of Perfection* and *The Interior Castle*.

Her friendship with John and her down to earth advice for her houses' rules for her fellow nuns show that she was no wooden saint but fully human and alive. The two first met when Teresa was 52 and beginning the foundation of her second reformed Carmel. John was 25 and a newly-ordained Carmelite priest. He was considering becoming a Carthusian and withdrawing from the world, but Teresa, in need of a counterpart to carry out a reform among the male communities of Carmelites, developed a friendship with him.

It is interesting to compare Teresa's personality to John's. While she was probably much more noticed in a room, both embraced holiness in their own way. She was a definite people-person. She was a born leader and took centre stage. Her manner of relating to others, whether circles of several persons or individuals, would look quite different from John's interactions. He tended to stay more in the background, but when called upon he was quite capable of exercising leadership and good management.[132]

Teresa came from a well-to-do background and was accustomed to eating fine foods. Some observers were appalled to see her dining on partridge, apparently scandalized that she would be enjoying herself so much.

'When I fast, I fast,' she retorted, 'and when I eat partridge, I eat partridge.' They probably didn't know that she used a log as a pillow, but asceticism is not something to be worn on one's sleeve. As she famously said: 'God save us from gloomy saints.'

She suffered greatly through sickness, persecution, trial by the Inquisition, being placed in 'voluntary retirement' and so on, leading her to remark to her Lord: 'If this is how you treat your friends, no wonder you have so many enemies.'

The famous saying 'Nade te turbe' is attributed to St Teresa of Avila. It is often referred to as 'St Teresa's Bookmark' as it was found written in the margins of her breviary after her death:

> Let nothing disturb you,
> Let nothing frighten you,
> All things are passing away:
> God never changes.
> Patience obtains all things.
> Whoever has God lacks nothing;
> God alone suffices.

Despite all this, she and John also knew how to rejoice together and with her fellow sisters. She speaks of their spiritual friendship when she writes in one of her letters: 'What a wonderful thing it is for two souls to understand each other, for they neither lack something to say, nor grow tired.'

In the famous seventh-century Egyptian 'Icon of friendship', Jesus is shown putting his arm around the shoulder of a friend – who perhaps represents each one of us. Jesus does not face his friend, rather He stands alongside him; He accompanies him, sharing in the burdens of life. In his left arm Jesus holds the Scriptures – the vital aid for spiritual friendship. The face of Jesus is kind: his eyes, large and open, are not severe or judgemental but gentle. His gaze is still, focused and intense. He looks beyond the world to his Father. Just as, with a gentle hand on the shoulder, Jesus guides his friend to contemplate in wonder the love of the Father for all, so does he guide us.[133]

One of the earliest people to define spiritual friendship is the English monk Aelred, who in 1147 became Abbot of Rievaulx near York. His short introduction *On Spiritual Friendship* became a classic. In it he speaks of friendship as 'agreement on all things sacred and profane accompanied by good will and love', a definition he borrowed from Cicero's 'De Amicitia'. A relationship of friendship helps us to grow in love for each other and love for God. Aelred writes in the form of a dialogue in which he says to his young friend Ivo: 'Here we are, you and I, and I hope a third, Christ is in our midst.' Aelred is asked: 'Could we say of friendship what John the friend of Christ says of Love, that God is friendship?' He replies that this would be unusual but it should be possible to say what is said of love: that 'those who abide in friendship abide in God and God in them'.[134] The person without a friend he likens to a beast who has no one with whom to rejoice, to whom to unburden one's heart, or with whom to share inspirations or great insights. A friend is one to whom, in equality and purity, we can confess our failings and make known our progress, and to whom we can trust all the secrets of our heart. This indeed is a help in the midst of the dark night.

Aelred discusses the qualities needed for friendship: loyalty, discretion, right intention and patience. He admits it is something we will experience with few people in this life, but we are called to develop friendships as a foretaste of many more in heaven, for as Jesus said: 'I do not call you servants, but friends.'

At a certain point in my life, I realized that work pressures and self-preoccupation had completely drowned out some former friendships that I now risked losing through neglect. It was during a Covid lockdown, when things slowed, that I began to renew and repair some ties of friendship. This was intentional and fruitful. But first it was challenging. Did I dare express to them my need for a friend? Would this be weird? Each conversation is different, and we need to know how to express a desire to establish friendships or whether simply to proceed and invest time needed without naming this. Whichever it may be, dear spiritual friend, is this a spiritual discipline you may consider investing in more?

The friendship combined with spiritual direction between Francis de Sales and Jane de Chantal in the early 1600s is another fine example of friendship through the night. This is particularly recorded in their brilliant letters.[135] Francis expresses himself with a frankness and brave affection which seems unguarded to us today in our age of safeguarding rules and boundaries. As he says: 'I am as human as anyone could possibly be.'[136] They met in 1604 when Jane was a young widow called to live a spiritual life. They did not often meet, and their deep friendship grew through their letters – an almost forgotten art today. Yet they contributed massively to the development of Spiritual Direction as we know it today. Francis as a bishop lived between Savoy in the east of France and the court in Paris, on whose service he was constantly travelling. Jane lived in Dijon and then near Reims. Together they invented the Order of the Visitation (in remembrance of Mary's famous visit to Elizabeth). This was a new way for women to live in community but go out into the world visiting the sick and those in need. By the time Jane died she had established 80 Visitation monasteries.

Henri Nouwen wrote a timely preface to these letters, saying:

> I am gradually becoming aware that our contemporary predicament allows us to find in these letters what is crucial for our own spiritual survival: a Jesus centred, affectionate friendship. This pervades all the letters that Francis and Jane write to all their correspondents, but the source is clearly the friendship between themselves.[137]

Let us take a glimpse at how they expressed themselves: On 24 June 1604, Francis writes to Jane:

> I want you to know that I have an intense and very special desire to serve you with all my strength. It would be impossible for me to explain either the quality or the greatness of this desire that I have to be at your service that I can tell you I believe it is from God, and for that reason I cherish it every day.[138]

It seems that the deep affection they have for each other is generously shared with all the women and men with whom they enter into a spiritual relationship. There is no holding back, no careful distance, no concern about the possible misinterpretations. There is a constant encouragement to be open, direct and spontaneous.

This is such a contrast to the rules of relating that pastors, leaders and spiritual directors will be very careful to observe today. Tragic stories of falls and failures of safeguarding have caused a complete rethink of boundaries and appropriate behaviour. This is necessary and right. However, the birth pains of this new way of doing things have for the moment seemed to place the Church almost in a straitjacket of distance, formality and remoteness. We do need a new way of safe behaviour, clearly. Past abuses have been so damaging. But the cost is great: people's capacity to dare to express loving care or commitment can be hampered.

Henri Nouwen concludes his Preface to these letters of friendship with an exhortation to dare to take risks:

> In a time in which there is so much concern about the right professional distance within a helping relationship and in which there is so much preoccupation with transference and countertransference, Jane de Chantal and Francis de Sales offer us fresh perspective on healing relationship. They dared to take risks with each other and those they cared for.[139]

We should probably make a distinction between Spiritual Friendship and Spiritual Direction. I believe we need both: with a spiritual director (ideally, everyone should have one) there will be less mutuality, though there may be some. This is, rather, a space for the directee not to be concerned about giving space to the other but rather to be able to express and describe their journey to someone who is listening. In spiritual friendship, however, there is mutual listening. Nouwen continues:

> 'Mutuality' is the word here. It is the mutuality of the Ministry of Jesus the good Shepherd who says, 'I know my own and my own know me.' A mutual openness, a mutual sharing, a mutual confession of needs, a mutual confession and forgiveness and mutual knowing and being known that is the source of a community – where God's strength is made manifest among a weak people.[140]

At any rate, perhaps this offers a different way forward to us today.

It is worth noting the 'de Sales spirituality' and atmosphere behind the friendship. There is fundamental optimism that 'the human person is made in the image of God'. There is a quest to discover 'God's happy will'. There is conviction that true spirituality does not have to retreat from people but is 'a life lived in the midst of the world'. There is a kind of spacious human liberty in the divine scheme of things. This is an indifference that frees people for the liberty of the children of God – and in an abandonment to holy providence. The letters speak not of external forms or religious practices or places but of inner transformation. Finally, we find an encouragement to do 'little things with great love'.

This is all refreshing and liberating in terms of friendship.[141]

As Francis de Sales begins the relationship, he writes: 'My very dear sister, be reassured that from the very beginning God gave me a tremendous love for yourself as you became more and more open with me and a marvellous obligation arose for my soul to love yours more and more.'[142]

He then goes on to discuss a large range of topics, including spiritual battle, having a French translation of her prayers 'so as to understand them better', whether Jane's daughter should become a nun ('if she wants to become one of her own accord, fine; otherwise, I do not approve of her being influenced by any recommendations'). He discusses a debt and when to pay it ('as soon as you can'), Jane's use of her time and care for her father and father-in-law ('I agree you should divide your time between them'). He moves on to more remarks on freedom ('constraint or slavishness is a certain lack of freedom that causes the soul to be unduly anxious or angry when it cannot carry out what it intended to do'). He gives several examples of freedom before closing with a beautiful exhortation to

> remember the day on which you took the crown of the kingdom of your own heart to lay it at the feet of Jesus, your King, the day on which you renewed your strength like an eagle's, the day that heralded the eternal day of your soul in the great resolution of belonging to God – body, heart and soul.[143]

Jane's letters to Francis have sadly been lost. But as an example of her friendship, she writes tenderly and in a similar way to one of her directees, her brother the Bishop of Bourges, about love for God being foremost and the need for abandonment to God's will, especially in times of loss. She writes: 'As often as you can in the day, unite your will to God's. Do this either be a simple loving glance at God, or by simple words such as "Yes Father", or "O Holy will of God live and rule in me".'[144]

Jane in fact lived a long season of Dark Night of the Soul, particularly as a result of bereavement when she lost her beloved husband, but also in other difficult landscapes. In addition, her friend Francis de Sales died 20 years before her, and she missed him cruelly. But spiritual friendships helped her to survive. She is instructive to us, giving a lesson on living in the now and in reality. She allowed into her discipline of abandonment to the will of God the very human, godly expression of sadness. She wrote to her brother on the occasion of Francis' death:

> you say you want to know what my heart felt on that occasion: truly I have never felt such an intense Grief nor has my heart ever received so great a blow ... My sorrow is greater than I could ever express, and it seems as though everything serves to increase my weariness. The only thing left to console me is to know that it is my God who permitted this blow to fall ... It's a terribly difficult exile for me, this miserable life. But I want to stay here as I said as long as it's God's plan for me.[145]

As I have said, it is a feature of mystics that far from being forever alone, they developed remarkable friendships. And Jane's correspondence is light, engaging, wise, cheerful and full of friendly encouragement.

Another who was gifted at friendship was Francis of Assisi. He was a shining light to an entire generation and still shines today. His spiritual practices of Contemplation and Silence, Poverty and Christlike lifestyle helping the poor turned a society on a hinge towards God. His love for creation and the environment influenced the artistic Renaissance, enabling artists to concentrate on real places and people in the sublime paintings they produced. Because of his love for the environment, expressed for example in Giotto's 'St Francis preaching to the birds' mural in Assisi Basilica, he became the patron saint of ecology. But one could say that his entire movement was founded on friendship. His closeness to his famous fellow-friars like Brothers Leo and Rufino and Angelo is remarkable. He also had a wonderful, devoted friendship with his directee St Clare. In their kindness to each other we see the deepest care and most passionate respect for one another without the slightest hint of eroticism. Perhaps there is some similarity here to the expectations we might have of a spiritual accompaniment relationship or in the Celtic tradition of the *anam cara* (literally, 'soul friend').

Dear spiritual friend, maybe you might at this time consider taking a friendship audit. Who are or who could be your spiritual friends?

As I have said, at a certain point I found, like Joseph in the desert, that I was 'looking for my brothers'. I found that they were far off, and I needed to act. If this is such a time for you, make contact if you can, renew relationships, listen and love and imitate Jesus who calls us to friendships. For some readers, the dark night is so dark as to have obliterated friends from view. But even if this is the case, we can talk about it with a trusted other – and pray about it. The trusted other may be a spiritual director, our spouse if we are married or another close to us. The fact is people are often looking for exactly this in our lonely world and we can be surprised by the response of some which will echo our feelings in this matter. In the end, as I have said, I reached out and said: 'Can we give some time to our friendship?' and heard a 'Yes' in return. It is a curious fact that to disclose oneself as vulnerable often provokes a response of warmth and compassion and affection – giving strength to journey on.

For Francis and Clare, friendship led to an experience of the Fire of God during a meal they took together, and we will return to this when after the Cloud and the Night we discuss mystical Fire …

But there is one more key that I observe to surviving the darkness, namely discovering the close nearness of God at the very centre of our beings. We now turn and pause for refreshment at this deep wayside well.

Mid-Point Resting Place on the Journey

© *Peronel Barnes, 'Provision'*

In the dark night there is provision. In the desert there is water. In the wilderness we may find an oasis. There is a hint in this image of the nail-pierced hand of Christ. Then there is abundant lifesaving water poured out, coming, it seems, from a fountain opened up.

On that day a fountain will be opened to the house of David and the inhabitants of Jerusalem, to cleanse them from sin and impurity. (Zech. 13.1)

We can be washed clean of trouble and sorrow and sin. We can find that he brings provision of peace, of strength for the journey, of hope for tomorrow.

I

Ways through the Darkness: Teresa of Avila and Finding the Still Centre

> I have seen the sun break through
> to illuminate a small field
> for a while, and gone my way
> and forgotten it. But that was the pearl
> of great price, the one field that had
> the treasure in it. I realize now
> that I must give all that I have
> to possess it. Life is not hurrying
>
> on to a receding future, nor hankering after
> an imagined past. It is the turning
> aside like Moses to the miracle
> of the lit bush, to a brightness
> that seemed as transitory as your youth
> once, but is the eternity that awaits you.
> (R. S. Thomas, 'The Bright Field')[146]

> Late have I loved you, beauty so old and so new: late have I loved you. And see, you were within and I was in the external world and sought you there, and in my unlovely state I plunged into those lovely created things which you made. You were with me, and I was not with you ... (Augustine, Confessions X.38)

> Well, let us consider this castle has, as I said 'many dwelling places' ...
> and in the centre and middle is the main dwelling place,
> where the very secret exchanges between God and the soul take place.
> (Teresa of Avila, *The Interior Castle*)[147]

We have reached the mid-point of our journey and we come aside to rest awhile. In fact, what we will explore is also a fourth way to help us through the Dark Night of the Soul. This is to discover the still place where God is and become one with him. To 'know' how to find the Comforter – through paths followed in the past – is another key to survival.

Some mystics believe in 'turning aside' like Moses to the miracle of the lit bush. They are arrested by moments of Glory. Elijah discovers God's presence on the mountain, after the wind and fire. Isaiah has a vision of God's glory filling the temple. Maybe part of their mystical preoccupation is that they notice and are enfolded into a profound, awesome sense of Union within creation. They also draw near to being aware in a new way of being sheltered within God's presence. They can experience transfixing, arresting flashes of Love when 'everything makes sense'. R. S. Thomas puts the mystics' longing well in his famous poem 'The Bright Field':

> Life is not hurrying
> on to a receding future ...
> It is the turning
> aside like Moses to the miracle
> of the lit bush ...
> the eternity that awaits you.[148]

And I believe this 'second sight' can become a spiritual practice.

But others, as in Augustine's 'Late have I loved you', the majestic passage from the Confessions quoted above, declare: 'you were within.' He finds God's presence within: 'you were within – and I was in the external world and sought you there ... You were with me, and I was not with you.'

The mystics have two different roadmaps to their destination of God's presence. Some search without and others look within. R. S. Thomas turns aside like Moses for that burning sight. *The Cloud of Unknowing* feels God as outside – beyond the cloud. 'Beat away at it', the writer says. 'Nothing matters now except that ... your naked being be carried gladly upwards in eagerness of love.'[149]

On the other hand, Augustine declares 'you were within'. Mme Guyon discovered: 'O my Lord, you were in my heart. You asked only that I should return within and feel your presence. O Infinite Goodness' and Teresa of Avila finds God within her 'Interior Castle'.[150]

The Bible gives merit to both: at the Mount of Transfiguration Jesus is enveloped in the Cloud coming from heaven above. But he also teaches that the kingdom of heaven is in our midst – or 'the kingdom of heaven is within you', as several translations have it.[151] It is, as Luther puts, it 'inwendig an euch' ('internally in you'). The Greek word *'entos'* ('within') probably means within us individually and also within us corporately as community. Paul later says: 'Do you not know that your bodies are temples of the Holy Spirit who is in you' (1 Cor. 6.19).

So it is that while many mystics seek God's presence in an Epiphany vision without, and find him in his creation, many also find him within, and this perhaps particularly during the dark night.

Dear spiritual friend, on this journey of longing and looking for God through the Cloud, the Night and through the Fire, it is good for us to ask: Do we have the reflex, the habit, the spiritual discipline to seek and recognize God's presence? And if so, do we apprehend this without or within? Then the question for me is: if it is without, do I 'beat away at this'? And if within, do I somehow seek to pass through the 'mansions' to the still centre of my interior castle, where God is? For myself, the answer is both. I look out, especially in the Cloud and the Night to his towering presence. I look inwards as well.

As already noted, this 'centre where God is' is not a concentration on or elevation of the self. It is an arresting awareness of God's Presence within. We experience what Jesus says of the Holy Spirit: 'He will be with you and he will be in you' (John 14.17), 'the kingdom of heaven is within you' (Luke 17.21). It is not a making of our inmost self in the image of God. But it is a finding of the presence of God in the deepest place of our soul – or 'deeper than the soul', as Teresa will have it. Augustine's well-known passage from the Confessions also contains finely tuned theology and is worth quoting in full:

> Late have I loved you, beauty so old and so new: late have I loved you.
> And see, you were within and I was in the external world and sought you there, and in my unlovely state I plunged into those lovely created things which you made. You were with me, and I was not with you. The lovely things kept me far from you, though if they did not have their existence in you, they had no existence at all. You called and cried out loud and shattered my deafness. You were radiant and resplendent, you put to flight my blindness. You were fragrant, and I drew in my breath and now pant after you. I tasted you, and I feel but hunger and thirst for you. You touched me, and I am set on fire to attain the peace which is yours.[152]

God was not to be found in the 'lovely created things' even though he made them. In the end, 'You called ... and shattered my deafness.' God called through his mother's prayers, his friendship with Ambrose of Milan and in the end through a child's voice saying, 'Take up and read.' Augustine testifies: 'You were within', 'You were with me', 'You were fragrant, and I drew in my breath.' He adds, in Song of Songs language, 'I now pant after you ... I am set on fire.' For Diarmaid MacCulloch, Augustine's impact on Western Christian thought can hardly be overstated – only his beloved example Paul of Tarsus has been more influential, and Westerners have generally seen Paul through Augustine's eyes. Here it is important to note that: Augustine is also a mystic – he also turns within and writes of being set on fire.[153]

Another contemplative to 'turn within' is Teresa of Avila. She wrote with pithy comparisons from everyday sights and events – a water reservoir, the soul like a ship at sea, a castle with a divine but unrecognized Guest. Her *Life* is rather like a blog or podcast, especially if listened to on audio rather than read. She returns, after different diversions, to ask: 'Now, where was I?' After describing these moments in her life of rejection, misunderstanding and occasional vindication she returns to her forensic analysis of how to make progress in our life of prayer.

Teresa is one who saw God's presence as residing inside our 'interior castle'. She has been credited, along with John of the Cross, as being one of the first to describe what has come to be known as 'Centring Prayer'.[154] It may well be that 'interior prayer' is a better name, a phrase drawn from her *Interior Castle*. But it is true that 'centring' may be more dynamic, implying movement towards the still centre.

Teresa's *Interior Castle* imagines our soul to be like a castle made entirely out of a diamond in which there are many rooms, just as in heaven there are many dwelling places. She says: 'Insofar as I can understand, the gate of entry to this castle is prayer and reflection.' She speaks of

> souls who in the end enter the castle. For even though they are very involved in the world, they have good desires sometimes ... they reflect on who they are. During the period of a month, they will sometimes pray – but their minds are then filled with business matters that ordinarily occupy them. They are so attached to these things that where their treasure is there their heart goes to. [In a graphic image she says:] Finally, they enter the first, lower rooms. But so many reptiles get in with them they are prevented from seeing the beauty of the castle and calming down: they have done quite a bit just by having entered.[155]

For her, so many 'reptiles' are being brought into our prayer space! This is not dissimilar to the person today who is attempting silence but is shipwrecked by their smartphone and constant distractions and background noise. Teresa is concerned, rightly, about the cleansing, purifying, concentrating attention required for the progress of the prayerful person towards union with God.

So it is that she helps us journey through all seven mansions toward union with God.

In her first book, *The Way of Perfection*, she writes of the first step, Recollection:

> It is called Recollection because the soul collects together all the faculties and enters within itself to be with its God. Its Divine Master comes more speedily to teach it, and to grant it the Prayer of Quiet, than in any other way ...
>
> Those who are able to shut themselves up in this way within this little Heaven of the soul, wherein dwells the Maker of Heaven and earth, and who have formed the habit of looking at nothing and staying in no place which will distract these outward senses, may be sure that they are walking on an excellent road, and will come without fail to drink of the water of the fountain, for they will journey a long way in a short time.[156]

Teresa likens this journey to that of a ship that has a good wind to go round the coast and goes much faster than those going by land.

> These souls have already ... put out to sea; though they have not sailed quite out of sight of land, they do what they can to get away from it, by recollecting their senses. If their recollection is genuine ... It is as if the soul were rising from play, for it sees that worldly things are nothing but toys; in due course it is like a person entering a strong castle, in order that it may have nothing more to fear from its enemies, that ... it cannot see them and the soul's spiritual sight becomes clear ...[157]

At our deepest interior, she says, the place is far from empty – we have there, in our interior castle, a Guest:

> If we took care always to remember what a Guest we have within us, I think it would be impossible for us to abandon ourselves to vanities and things of the world, for we should see how worthless they are by comparison with those which we have within us.[158]

She returns often to the decision to want to live a holy life and to put away all sinful temptation and habits. This is common to all true mystics. This done, God expands and 'enlarges our heart' (Psalm 119.32).

> Gradually he enlarges our heart to the extent required for what he has to set within it ... He has power to make the whole of this palace great. The important point is that we should be absolutely resolved to give it to him for his own ... so that he may take out and put in just what he likes. If we fill the palace with vulgar people and all kinds of junk, how can the Lord and his Court occupy it?[159]

As we exercise this prayer of Recollection we find our heart beginning to fill up and this moves us on to another stage, the Prayer of Quiet, with the soul as a reservoir.

Teresa describes the place within us that is 'deeper than the soul' as a reservoir that can be filled with water in two ways: one by complex means of water-carrying and conduits made by human ingenuity, and the other as if a spring is already within the reservoir and fills it imperceptibly and without effort and leads to overflowing water. She says:

> Water-carrying corresponds to the spiritual sweetness which, as I say, is produced by meditation. It reaches us by way of the thoughts; we meditate upon created things and fatigue the understanding; and when at last, by means of our own efforts, it comes, the satisfaction which it brings to the soul fills the basin, as I have said.
>
> To the other fountain the water comes direct from its source, which is God, and, when it is His Majesty's will and he is pleased to grant us some supernatural favour, its coming is accompanied by the greatest peace and quietness and sweetness within ourselves – I cannot say where it arises or how. And that content and delight are not felt ... in the heart – I mean not at the outset. But later the basin becomes completely filled, and then this water begins to overflow all the Mansions and faculties, until it reaches the body.[160]

The heavenly water begins to flow from this source – that is from our very depths – and proceeds to spread within us and cause 'ineffable blessings, so that the soul itself cannot understand all that it receives there'.

Ezekiel had a vision of water flowing from the temple and growing deeper and bringing life and healing further afield. If we read this in a contemplative way, and particularly if we apply this to our own body, our spiritual temple of the Holy Spirit, this irrigation floods us and then, God willing, flows outwards: 'where the river flows, everything shall live' (Ezek. 47.9). As Jesus said: 'Let anyone who is thirsty come to me and drink. Whoever believes in me, as Scripture has said, rivers of living water will flow from within them' (John 7.37–38).

Teresa changes the metaphor from water to fire, for she is speaking of the Holy Spirit:

> The fragrance it experiences, we might say, is as if in those interior depths there were a brazier on which were cast sweet perfumes; the light cannot be seen, nor the place where it dwells, but the fragrant smoke and the heat penetrate the entire soul, and very often, as I have said, the effects extend even to the body.[161]

She says that we become absorbed and are amazed as we consider what is happening to us. She continues:

> Now, daughters, I still want to describe this Prayer of Quiet to you, ...
>
> This is a supernatural ... state in which the Lord gives it peace through his presence, as he did to that just man Simeon. In this state all the faculties are stilled. The soul realizes that it is now very close to God, and that, if it were but a little closer, it would become one with him through union ... The just man Simeon saw no more than the glorious Infant – a poor little Child ... But the Child Himself revealed to him Who he was. Just so, though less clearly, does the soul know Who he is.[162]

For her, the soul is near to the King who will give it the Kingdom. For her the soul is

> as it were, in a swoon, both inwardly and outwardly, so that the outward 'body' does not wish to move, but rests, like one who has almost reached the end of his journey, so that it may the better start again upon its way, with redoubled strength for its task.[163]

The body experiences the greatest delight, and the soul is conscious of a deep satisfaction:

> So glad is it merely to find itself near the fountain that, even before it has begun to drink, it has had its fill. There seems nothing left for it to desire. The faculties are stilled and have no wish to move, for any movement they may make appears to hinder the soul from loving God.[164]

Dear spiritual friend, we draw near to the Beauty of the silence of the Glory of God, and he is the Wonderful Counsellor as well as the Comforter who 'lightens our darkness'.

Teresa, of course, goes on to recommend silence, speaking disparagingly of those who 'deafen their ears to his voice' by going on talking and repeating a large number of vocal prayers 'which only distract them from their purpose'.

By contrast she speaks of 'Quiet':

> They are in the palace, near to their King, and they see that he is already beginning to give them his Kingdom on earth. Sometimes tears come to their eyes, but they weep very gently and quite without distress: their whole desire is the hallowing of this name. They seem not to be in the world, and have no wish to see or hear anything but their God; nothing distresses them, nor does it seem that anything can possibly do so. In short, for as long as this state lasts, they are so overwhelmed and absorbed by the joy and delight.[165]

After the Prayer of Quiet there comes 'Union'. As is often said, effort will not achieve this but only an act of God. Teresa quotes the Song of Songs again:

> I was struck by the words of the Bride in the Song of Songs, which you will remember hearing: 'The King brought me into the cellar of wine':[166] she does not say she went of her own accord, although telling us how she wandered up and down seeking her Beloved.
>
> I think the prayer of union is the 'cellar' in which our Lord places us when and how he chooses, but we cannot enter it through any effort of our own. His Majesty alone can bring us there and come into the centre of our souls ... He does not require the faculties or senses to open the door to him; they are all asleep. He enters the innermost depths of our souls without a door, as he entered the room where the disciples sat, saying 'Pax vobis' (Peace be with you) as he emerged from the sepulchre without removing the stone that closed the entrance.[167]

In this description of what I have called 'Finding the still centre', these mystics are pointing to our inheritance and destiny. They are experiencing what the Apostle Paul described as 'Christ in you, the hope of Glory'. This is the Apostle Peter's 'we are partakers of the Divine Nature'. This is recognizing Jesus' 'The Kingdom of Heaven is within you' and 'He will be with you and he will be in you.'

Another mystic to speak of this mystery within of Union with God is the great Julian of Norwich. Like Teresa, a journey of cleansing from sin and renouncing it has been experienced prior to Union. Julian of Norwich speaks of this in her graphic visions of the might and power of the cleansing stream of healing from Christ crucified: 'the precious plenty of his dearworthy blood ascended up into heaven'. In such arresting ways she saw his drying blood and 'the changing of colour of his fair face in token of his dearworthy passion'.[168]

Julian is one who saw God as without and also as within. She underlined the fact that our inheritance is indeed to be *oned* with him, as she puts it. Her 'Revelations of Divine Love' are just that – remarkable 'Shewings' concerning God's deep love for humankind expressed in Jesus and his passion in which he defeated 'the Fiend'. As one gets to know the Revelations, one finds oneself in the middle of a great scheme – a network of ideas that crisscross and interweave in a way that, though not clear at first reading, are all beautifully held together by the thread of 'dearworthy Love'. Fifteen years after her revelations she concludes with her famous words:

> Wouldst thou know thy Lord's meaning in this thing? Learn it well: Love was his meaning. Who shewed it thee? Love. What shewed he thee? Love. Wherefore shewed it he? For Love ... Thus was I learned that Love was our Lord's meaning.[169]

And this careful journey has – perhaps inevitably – this same destination: Union with God. She writes at her midpoint too:

> And I saw no difference between God and our Substance: but as it were all God ... our Substance is in God: that is to say that God is God and our Substance is a creature in God.[170]

She goes on to speak of the Almighty Truth of the Trinity being our Father; that the Deep Wisdom of the Trinity is our Mother; and that the High Goodness of the Trinity is our Lord – saying that in these three 'we are all enclosed', meaning union with God:

> We are enclosed in the Father, we are enclosed in the Son and we are enclosed in the Holy Ghost. And the Father is enclosed in us, the Son is enclosed in us and the Holy Ghost is enclosed in us; Almightiness, All-Wisdom, All-Goodness: one God, one Lord.[171]

She speaks too, like so many mystics, of our Union with God and his dwelling in us – a both-and relationship that is fruitful to dwell on, concluding:

> For it is nothing else but a right understanding, and a true belief, and a sure trust of our Being, that we are in God and God is in us, whom we see not. And this virtue, with all other that God has ordained to us cometh therein and works in us great things ... through the gifts and the virtues of the Holy Ghost.[172]

If we ask the question 'How does this work?' we return to Teresa to see that she describes Union in different ways:

> It may be symbolized by two wax candles, the tips of which touch each other so closely that there is but one light; or again, the wick, the wax, and the light become one, but the one candle can again be separated from the other and the two candles remain distinct; or the wick may be withdrawn from the wax.[173]

For her, spiritual marriage is like rain falling from heaven into a river or stream, becoming one and the same liquid, so that the river and rain water cannot be divided; or like a stream flowing into the sea, which cannot afterwards be disunited from it.

It is like a room into which a bright light enters through two windows – though divided when it enters, the light becomes one and the same. She writes:

> Perhaps when St. Paul said, 'He who is joined to the Lord becomes one spirit with him' (1 Cor. 6.17), he meant this sovereign marriage, which presupposes His Majesty having been joined to the soul by union. The same Apostle says: 'To me, to live is Christ and to die is gain.' This, I think, might here be uttered by the soul ... for Christ is her life.[174]

Interior or Centring Prayer

I have dwelt on the stages of 'interior' or centring prayer at some length because people are often simply defeated by the attempt to find solitude and silence, stillness and presence.[175]

Almost every week I speak with people who see the value of silence but are completely unable to achieve it without the brain flying off in different directions. It is almost as if being present in the silence is now an impossibility. How can we respond if this is the case?

The brain has a complexity that is truly staggering. Scientists have now found that in a one cubic millimetre speck of brain, amounting to one millionth of the whole brain, there are roughly 57,000 cells and 150 million neural pathways. 'It's a little bit humbling,' says Dr Viran Jain, 'How are we going to come to terms with all that complexity?'[176] This is perhaps why slowing down the brain, that miraculous organism, and concentrating and being present in the silence is such a counter-intuitive challenge.

And yet. And yet, we *can* 'Be still and know that he is God'. It may indeed be that we *must* 'Be still to know'. We need to grow our strength: and just like an athlete I believe we can consciously increase our holding power, our capacity, day by day for more seconds – then more minutes – of silence. Often what is needed, as I have said, is to grow the muscles of being present.

As a soul-building contemplation work-out, one exercise routine that I recommend as helpful is to give time — say five minutes each by the clock – to each of the three stages: Recollection, Quiet, and then Union and Communion: so, fifteen minutes each day for thirty days. I have become aware of the Ignatian virtue of repetition and so make no apology for recommending an exercise for repetition, or repeating myself in what can be the content for this. As I say, think of this as exercise – muscle-building for the art of Stillness. It may seem banal, but I use a timer for this – just like an athlete trying to increase capacity. And the results are rewarding. Because we are incarnational beings our posture can help, though discard this if it is not helpful! For what it's worth, it may be good to sit with both feet on the ground and your hands on your knees, a straight back and a relaxed body ... to call all your thoughts home. Gradually you will be present in the moment to God. It takes practice to begin with, of course.

Then turn your hands over in an attitude of receiving and, for another five minutes, again pay attention to your breathing, This is now the stage of the 'Prayer of Quiet' – a listening stillness. Listen to God's living Word, spoken out of the silence. This may be a remembering of scripture already read that day – a turning over in your thinking and some meditation on the Word. But it is often completely new.

Lastly, for a final five minutes, it may help to move your hand to cover your heart and wait for Union, aspiring and looking to be filled with God's presence and his peace. This could be the place to pray that 'small word' (God, Love, Beloved ...) as described above by *The Cloud of Unknowing*. Or it may be a time for complete silence.

We remember that Paul wrote to the Ephesians praying 'that you may be filled to the measure of all the fullness of God' (Eph. 3.19).

So I believe that then the miracle of Union may come to us.

What does this entail? Many things of course.

Teresa of Avila speaks of 'stretching' our understanding to inviting and being aware even of God the Holy Trinity within us: the spirit becomes enkindled and is illumined by a cloud of the greatest brightness. It sees these three persons individually. And yet the soul realizes that all these three persons are one substance and one Power and one knowledge and one God alone ... Julian of Norwich agrees, saying: 'Where Jesus is spoken of, the Holy Trinity is always to be understood.'[177]

In the biblical book of Revelation, the church in Laodicea is told of Christ saying he stands at the door and knocks. 'If anyone opens the door, I will come in and eat with that person and they with me' (Rev. 3.20). I find it helpful to understand that in fact the whole of the Trinity will enter and be within. We will get more than we bargained for.

I'm reminded of a story of a man who got engaged to marry the daughter of a billionaire. His future father-in-law asked him what he would like for a wedding present. Knowing his father-in-law's wealth and pitching his request reasonably moderately, the man replied: 'I would love some new golf clubs if that were possible.' Months went by and the eve of the wedding arrived. The father-in-law took the bridegroom on one side and said: 'I'm so sorry not to give you your golf clubs yet. The trouble is I want all of them to have swimming pools, and can so far only find a couple that do, which I have bought for you – but I will find more clubs with pools in the future and give them to you, I promise.' Here the man got a lot more than he bargained for. And in the mystical world, so may we.

Teresa even says that when she is at this stage, she experiences 'loving desire to leave this exile and return [i.e. to die and be with Christ]', but she offers 'to His Majesty the desire to live as the most costly offering'. She says: 'there is a great detachment in everything ... The soul is fortified by the strength it has from drinking wine in this wine cellar ... strength flows back.'

She was an active contemplative, always balancing the interior life with service of others:

Do you think that your service of people is of little benefit? The fire enkindles their soul ... the Lord doesn't look so much at the greatness of our works as at the love with which they are done. His Majesty will enable us to do more and more each day. During the shortness of this life, let us offer to God interiorly and exteriorly the sacrifice we can.[178]

So it is that as centring prayer becomes part of us, we will be empowered to move to mission, action and service – to move through it to love given away for others.

Union with God

Dear spiritual friend, this goal of the mystical approach is one experience all humankind longs for, I believe, for we are created for God. Augustine's 'Thou hast made us for thyself and our hearts are restless till they find their rest in Thee' is oft-quoted but seldom practised. It may be that few find real rest daily in God.

Beloved friend in God, consider your life. Many people are rushing or worrying or striving, while our whole being is maybe yearning for 'soul rest'. This is the Holy Longing for Union that can heal our alienation on earth. I believe we can and must make room for it – room for him.

We are often like electric vehicles which never make time to park up and plug in. By definition, for the vehicle this takes a time of stillness. Without this the vehicle will run out of energy and come to a stop. Some people come to an abrupt stop through breakdown or burn-out. But many others just lose joy and gradually find they are living as if on a permanent, tiring treadmill – even though they may not yet have come to a stop. Still they 'have gone on living, living and partly living' as T. S. Eliot put it.[179]

Through the cross Jesus brings to humankind peace with God. He gives relationship a completely new focus and destiny and even drive to work for his kingdom to come on earth as in heaven. He brings consolation in our troubles. The father sends his Holy Spirit upon us for this comfort and also to give power to continue and be fruitful. We can practise the presence of God which is a key to everything.

But he also calls us to abide.

Arguably the world still waits for people who have learnt to abide, to remain and to work out of a place of stillness.

'Be still and know that I am God!' says the psalmist – for this we may need to practise the art of stillness daily. (Psalm 46.10)

'Abide in me and I in you,' says Jesus – for this we learn we may need daily to 'find the place of abiding'. (John 15.4)

'We will come to him and make our home with him,' he says – for this we may need regularly to recognize, make space for, the one who is in our 'interior castle'. (John 14.23)

'I pray ... that you may be filled with all the fullness of God,' says Paul – his filling up of our interior pool can become a daily discipline too. (Eph. 3.19)

This is resting in God, communing with God and becoming 'oned' with him by grace. I believe this is helped by the steps described above.

The content of Union and Communion with God is hard to describe. It may be indescribable without poetry, as we have seen. It is comprised of everything described in this book and much more.

'God made Himself man so that man might become God' is a powerful sentence found in Irenaeus, then Athanasius, Gregory of Nyssa and so on, echoing through the writings of the Church Fathers. This gave rise to the term *theosis*. I have not included here a discussion of how the word *'theosis'* developed in Church history. The Orthodox Church translates this variously as *deification* or *divinization.* Nor have I discussed how the Orthodox Church sees the route to this differently to the Western Church. For myself, I prefer to translate *theosis* as 'Union and Communion with God'. As I have said, to enter a forensic discussion of this is too dense a theme for the purpose of this book. I refer the interested reader to some further study.[180]

My concern has been to say that the benefits of Mystical Union are very, very many: happiness, peace, healthy and holy detachment; and, in the long term, as we leave this space, Christlike fruitfulness: love, joy, peace, patience, kindness, goodness, faithfulness, gentleness and self-control. Union and Communion also involve empowering, refining and consuming fire. We gladly move now into this third landscape of the mystical journey through life: the Fire of God.

PART 3

The Fire

© *Peronel Barnes, 'Winterlight'*

We witness the possibility of light – fire breaking forth from the depths of winter darkness. The painting has a circular shape of dynamic light streaking out from its centre.

There are hints of birds' wings reminding me of T. S. Eliot's line evoking the day of Pentecost: 'The dove descending breaks the air with flame of incandescent terror.'[181] And once the fire comes, it illuminates the edge of the canvas with textured beauty.

I

Richard Rolle the Forerunner

For love ... burns like blazing fire, like a mighty flame. (Song 8.6)

And I saw a shining fire, unfathomable, inextinguishable, fully alive and existing full of life; with a flame the colour of the air, brightly burning in the gentle breeze ... And suddenly a dark sphere of air appeared, huge in size, upon which the shining flame struck many blows, and at each blow a spark flew up so that soon the circle of air was brought to completion, and heaven and earth shone forth in the fullness of perfection. (Hildegard of Bingen's twelfth-century 'Visions of the Creation')[182]

Ite Inflammate Omnia (Go and set the world on Fire)
(Ignatius of Loyola's customary way of signing letters to his Jesuits)

What mortal man could survive that heat at its peak as we can know it even here, if it persisted. He must inevitably wilt before the vastness and sweetness of love so fervid and heat so indescribable. (Richard Rolle)[183]

The journey of the one looking for God will at some point be confronted ... by fire!

- Moses' journey begins with an angel appearing 'in flames of fire'.
- God guides the people to freedom in 'a pillar of cloud and fire'.
- The glory of God was a 'consuming fire on top of the mountain'.
- The Songs of Songs says: 'Love burns like blazing fire.'
- Ezekiel sees 'fire and brilliant light surrounding him'. The record of this encounter says: 'Such was the appearance of the likeness of the glory of the Lord.'
- John the Baptist prophesied: 'He will baptize you with ... fire.'

- The book of Hebrews says: 'Our God is a consuming Fire.'
- Jesus said: 'I have come to bring fire on the earth, and how I wish it was already kindled.'[184]

Since those days of inspiration and epiphany, many people have testified to experiencing a sight of Fire. Within the Cloud and the Night, people have experienced Fire.

It can be the fire of suffering, the fire of refining, the fire of empowering, the fire giving courage. In the end, entering and being in the Fire of God is the surprisingly common story of many mystics old and new.

Hildegard of Bingen, who has become the patron saint of music, writing and ecology, back in the twelfth century had her famous vision described above in which she saw the whole of Creation conceived in Fire which illuminated and fanned her life into flame. She 'heard a voice speaking to her from the living fire: 'though you are a woman uneducated ... nevertheless you are touched by my light, which touches your inner being with fire like the burning sun. Shout and Tell. And write down these mysteries which you see and hear in the mystical vision. Do not be afraid, but tell.' This light touching our inner being 'with fire like the burning sun' is a dramatic image indeed. As we shall see, it has been echoed through the centuries.

The fourteenth and fifteenth centuries are called the 'Golden Age of English Mysticism',[185] and at the heart of this was the great Richard Rolle. He describes and explores the experience of fire, heat, love and sweetness that can follow the cloud and the night. His great work from the 1300s, *The Fire of Love* (*Incendium Amoris*) begins boldly:

> I cannot tell you how surprised I was the first time my heart began to warm. It was real warmth too ... I felt as if I actually was on fire. I was astonished at how the heat surged up and how this new sensation brought great and unexpected comfort ... Before the infusion of this comfort, I had never thought that we exiles could know such warmth, so sweet was the devotion that it kindled. It set my heart on fire as if a real fire was burning there.[186]

Rolle's writing is beautiful and lucid. He moves beyond intellectual thoughts about God to burning emotion: 'I call it fervour when the mind is truly ablaze with eternal love, and the heart similarly feels itself burning with a love that is not imaginary but real. For a heart set on fire produces a feeling of fiery love.'[187]

He was born into a farming family sometime around 1300. It is possible that at some point he travelled to France and studied at the Sorbonne, perhaps taking a master's degree. He may also have been ordained there. He attended Oxford, studying philosophy, theology and the Bible. It seems he was dissatisfied with the emphasis of the academic life, and left Oxford without completing his degree to seek God alone. About three years into his solitary life Rolle began to have mysterious encounters which would become the foundation of his life.

Rolle looked to have an imaginative prayer life. At the same time, he wrote about contemplative prayer. His writings are deeply personal. He describes his personal suffering as he entered the way.[188] And then, as Evelyn Underhill wrote: 'It was brought to an end, as with so many of the greater mystics, by an abrupt shifting of consciousness to levels of peace and joy: a sudden and overwhelming revelation of Spiritual Reality – "the opening of the heavenly door, that Thy face showed".'[189]

After this, Rolle passed to that experience of God's presence which he calls the 'Fire': the state that includes the three experiences, or spiritual moods, of Calor, Dulcor and Cantor (Heat, Sweetness and Song). At the end of a year, 'the door biding open ... I sat forsooth in a chapel and whilst with sweetness of prayer or meditation muckle I was delighted, suddenly in me I felt a merry heat before this time unknown.'[190]

He joins other mystics in calling people away from the chatter and 'the racket' into the silent land: we cannot get away from this as a pathway – a road less travelled – towards encounter and, indeed, the fire of love. He writes: 'I have found that to love Christ above all else will involve three things: warmth and song and sweetness. And these as I know from experience cannot exist without here being great quiet.'[191]

The Fire of Love

When we ask what Rolle really meant by this image of the fire of love, we stand on the threshold of exploring a beautiful new land. This is one of those phrases, half metaphor, so apt that we could also call them descriptions of experience, which are natural to mystical literature. Immemorially old yet eternally fresh, they appear again and again, and these reappearances are not due to conscious borrowing. The fire of love is a term that goes back at least to the fourth century; it is used by St Macarius of Egypt to describe the action of the Divine Energy upon the soul that it is leading to perfection.

Its origins are of course described in the Bible – the fusion of St John's 'God is love' with the fire imagery of the Hebrew prophets. 'Behold! the Lord will come with fire!' 'His word was in my heart as a burning fire.' 'He is like a refiner's fire.' The experience reminds us of John the Baptist's promise: 'He will baptize you with the Holy Spirit – and with Fire.' The disciples on the road to Emmaus ask themselves: 'Did not our hearts burn within us as he talked with us on the road and opened the scriptures to us?' And on the day of Pentecost itself there is the warming, burning visitation of 'tongues of Fire that separated and came to rest on each of them'. For Rolle there is the wound of the fire, the Union with God in the fire. But over all there is always the Johannine lived experience that 'God is Love'.[192]

In the passages in which Rolle speaks of that 'Heat' which the Fire of Love induced in his purified heart turned towards heaven, we see that this means a felt, embodied as well as spiritual experience. Those interior states or moods are given names: 'Heat, Sweetness and Song'. They are echoed in the bodily experience of many mystics and later, forerunner leaders such as Pascal, George Fox, George Whitefield and John Wesley, and their American contemporary Johnathan Edwards, leader of the Great Awakening and sometime President of Princeton. These were among the leading thinkers of their day. Then, in what one might call a great democratizing and levelling, Fire fell at Azusa Street, Los Angeles, at the start of the twentieth century upon first nations people, people of colour including former slaves and the poor – bringing about the birth of Pentecostalism and, through the Charismatic movement, its spread into almost all Christian denominations.

To return to Rolle's time, he wrote:

I long for love, the fairest of flowers, and inwardly burn with fiery flame ... The heat is such that no one can imagine it unless he has experienced its comfort for himself. His heart is bursting with song, a captive in the care of charity. For of all the things I experience here, this is the most delightful: I nearly die while it builds up its fervent love.[193]

In a truly loving mind, there is always a song of glory and an inner flame of love. They surge up out of a clear conscience, out of an abundance of inward gladness. Small wonder if a love like this wins through to a perfect love. Love of this sort is immense in its fervour and its whole direction Godwards totally unrestrained in its love for him.[194]

The Wound of Love

For Rolle there is joy, delight, fervent love and song. But Rolle also says: 'I nearly die while it builds up' and speaks of the 'inner flame of love'. He is in the company of later writers like Teresa of Avila, John of the Cross and many others and, of course, before him the writer of the Song of Songs. There we read of the Bride who is 'sick with love' and of love that 'burns like holy fire'.[195] He experiences the 'affective wound' caused by the flame of divine love referred to in the Song of Songs: 'I am wounded with love.'

'A lover will languish if he does not have the object of his love near him,' says Rolle, which is why scripture says: 'Tell my Beloved I languish for love', as if it were saying:

> It is because I cannot see him, my very body is wasting away with the intensity of my devotion ... when one pines for love, and is carried away by it, one can say, 'I languish for love.' For it is thus that a man regards his Beloved. He forgets himself and everything else for Christ's sake.[196]

John of the Cross uses the phrase 'The Living Flame of Love' as the title for his final great work. He writes:

> O severe burn
> O delicious wound
> O tender hand! O gentle touch
> That savours of eternal life,
> And pays every debt!
> In slaying you have changed death to life.[197]

In human love stories, we speak of a person being 'lovesick'. Quite a good earthly comparison is when someone finds and falls in love with their 'Beloved-for-life', is 'wounded with love', and gladly dies to every other romantic love and cannot rest until marriage comes. It can sometimes be that if death or any other reason parts them, they find themselves for ever wounded and ruined.

For a mother or father, their new-born, longed-for child may wound with healing love, gladly leading to care that will last a lifetime. But then, if there is estrangement, it can be a living death.

These are images or previews, echoing our longing for God who is our ultimate Beloved. John of the Cross's poem describes the real drama, joy and pain of the divine romance:

> Thus the divine burn of love heals the wound that love has caused and by each application renders it greater. The healing love brings is to wound again what was wounded before, until the soul melts away in the fire of Love ... transformed in love, wounded with love. For herein he who is most wounded is the most healthy, and he who is all wound is all health.[198]

This is completely paradoxical and contradictory. But it has been well said (by G. K. Chesterton among others) that any account of Christianity that does not include paradox risks falling into heresy. So this 'fatal wound of love' is something Richard Rolle knows.

Dear spiritual friend, do you know something of this? Is it part of the mystical journey today? I came across this as a modern reality when serving for ten years in a French-speaking church in Belleville, Paris. Paris is the capital of perfume and romance, and at that time I learnt a lot about passionate love for God from French Christians. One of several contemporary French worship songs we sang included the verse:

> *Tu es le plus beau*
> *de tous les fils de l'homme,*
> *Tu déploies sur moi ton amour,*
> *Et la grâce qui coule de tes lèvres*
> *Est un baume,*
> *Un baume de vie et un baume d'amour.*
> *Oui je suis malade, malade d'amour.*
> (I am faint with love, sick with love)[199]

In those days we also served a ministry that gathered around 2,500 Catholics and Protestants at an annual event whose name was 'Embrase nos coeurs' – literally: 'Set our hearts on fire.'

This love-sickness or wound of love is described by Teresa of Avila. Teresa's practical nature allowed her to describe and analyse her experiences with unparalleled concreteness in her famous *Life* and other books that followed:

I saw in his hand a long spear of gold, and at the point there seemed to be a little fire. He appeared to me to be thrusting it at times into my heart, and to pierce my very entrails; when he drew it out, he seemed to draw them out also, and to leave me all on fire with a great love of God. The pain was so great, that it made me moan; and yet so surpassing was the sweetness of this excessive pain, that I could not wish to be rid of it. The sweetness caused by this intense pain is so extreme that one cannot possibly wish it to cease, nor is one's soul then content with anything but God. This is not a physical, but a spiritual pain, though the body has some share in it – even a considerable share. So gentle is this wooing which takes place between God and the soul that if anyone thinks I am lying, I pray God in his goodness, to grant him some experience of it.[200]

Today, since Freud, there is a 'hermeneutic of suspicion' through which any passage including words like 'thrust' and 'moan' has inevitably to pass! But I don't feel Teresa's description is erotic displacement language, any more than what we find in the Song of Songs itself.

Anyway, Teresa's practical gifts and achievements no doubt made this experience believable, however challenging it may have seemed. So much was it believed that a hundred years later it was carved in Rome by Bernini into the marble of his exquisite life size statue of the event. Her experience of this fiery point of a lance being thrust into her heart was a very painful encounter, but the result of it, she says, is the sweetness – 'so as to leave me all on fire with a great love of God'.

We will speak more of 'Eros and Allegory' later and in the following note. But suffice it to say that human love stories and human erotic experience, wonderful as they are, can also be seen as paler shadows of the even more real, bright love affair with God. They can point back and forward to the Shining Source of all Love – a greater and truer passion, love and union. Hence writers sometimes borrow amorous and erotic language because it is the best parallel and imaginative language we can find to hand.[201]

In an echo of this, in *The Cloud of Unknowing* we read:

Sometimes God may send out a ray of divine light, piercing this cloud of unknowing between you and him and letting you see some of his ineffable mysteries. You'll feel on fire with his love then. I can't describe this experience. It's beyond words. My foolish, human tongue can't describe God's grace. Even if I dared, I would refuse, and that's that.[202]

Another wounded mystic was the great Jeanne Guyon (1648–1717), who after a critical time of searching was told by her spiritual director that she was seeking outside herself that which she had within. She should, he said, accustom herself to seek God in her heart and she would find him. She felt these words like an 'arrow which pierced my heart through and through'. The following morning, she describes what happened when she came to prayer:

> I felt in this moment *a profound wound* which was full of delight and love – *a wound so sweet* that I desired that it would never heal ... O my Lord, you were in my heart. You asked only that I should return within and feel your presence. O Infinite Goodness.[203]

This 'wound so sweet she thought it would never heal' is noteworthy. Through her beloved writing 'Experiencing the Depths of Jesus Christ' she still moves and encourages those seeking God today, perhaps particularly French Protestants. Jeanne suffered an unhappy forced marriage and then months of persecution, threat and prison as her ideas appeared to encourage the bypassing of the clergy to approach God directly through Christ. In 'Experiencing the Depths', first published in 1685 as '*Moyen court et facile de faire oraison*' ('A short and very easy method of Prayer which all can practise'), she tells her readers that although most Christians do not feel that they have been called to a deep inward relationship to Jesus Christ, in fact we have all been called to the depths of Christ just as surely as we have been called to salvation.

She says: 'Actually it is very simple. It is only a turning and yielding of your heart to the Lord. It is an expression of love within your heart for him.' Many of the key themes of quiet leading to Contemplation are explored with down-to-earth, and in my view helpful, instructions. In the end she speaks of the nearness of God's felt presence:

> Do not try to say anything. Do not try to do anything: Just remain there ... You should not seek to move as long as he is near. When the awareness of his presence eventually begins to decrease – utter some words of love to God or simply call on his name: you will immediately be brought back to the sweetness of his presence. What is the point? The point is this: *there is a fire* which fades and grows. The fire, when it fades, must be gently fanned, but only gently. Just as soon as that fire begins to burn, again cease all your efforts. Otherwise, you might put out the flame.[204]

Perhaps we can pause to let our hearts also be moved by this call to go deeper, to stir up rather than put out this flame.

The Fire of Suffering

We pause to note that the wound of the fire of love may feel for some more like the Fire of Suffering.

This burning heat of life's troubles and sorrows is common to all our lives, and a frequent question is: Where then is God in it? He seems absent, so can we somehow compare suffering with the wound of God's Love?

The mystics take the bold view that all events in our lives come from God who is sovereign, as Julian of Norwich says: 'And I saw that truly nothing happens by accident or luck, but everything by God's wise providence.'

This is tough, very tough, but ultimately true, I believe. It sounds like a foreign language to our generation, including to me – but in the end, acceptance and reconciling oneself to God within the fire and to his permissive will and ultimate new creation may save us from burning up in bitterness or from the ravages of rejection of God. One pathway for me in any burning suffering is therefore to cling on to God even if this also burns.

For help in this, I turn to the mystical poetry of T. S. Eliot. After the ravages and 'Waste Land' of the First World War, Eliot became reconciled to faith in Christ, famously falling to his knees in front of Michelangelo's 'Pieta' sculpture of Jesus on a visit to St Peter's in Rome in 1926. He describes something similar to this wound towards the end of the *Four Quartets*. There he makes references to Julian of Norwich's comforting and radical words: 'All shall be well.' But before this, there is the fire of suffering and the wound of fire. Eliot writes:

> The dove descending breaks the air
> With flame of incandescent terror
> Of which the tongues declare
> The one discharge from sin and error ...
> Who then devised the torment? Love.
> Love is the unfamiliar Name.[205]

It is as if connection with the Divine – even being discharged from sin – is a fiery process of death to all things except God. The Dove of the fiery Holy Spirit and then 'tongues' is not a comfortable comforter for Eliot. Images in the background of this scene may have to do with the incandescent terror of the bombs of the recent war.[206] But also the Fire of Love is a severe mercy, it seems. Eliot calls it a 'torment', continuing: 'Who then devised the torment? Love. Love is the unfamiliar Name.'

This is a stark adaptation of Julian of Norwich's more comforting conclusion at the very end of her *Revelations of Divine Love*:

> What, do you wish to know your Lord's meaning in this thing? Know it well, love was his meaning.
> Who reveals it to you? Love. What did he reveal you? Love.
> Why does he reveal it to you? For Love …
> So I was taught that love is our Lord's meaning.[207]

The fact is, though, that Julian of Norwich herself had suffered sickness, hunger and poverty. She had lived through plague and pestilence. It was from this context that she reached her famous conclusion: 'It was necessary that there should be sin, but all shall be well, and all shall be well, and all manner of things shall be well.'[208] Eliot concludes his great poem 'Little Gidding'[209] in a similar way. After his famous encouragement that the end of all our exploring will be to return to where we started and 'know the place for the first time', he concludes that what is needed is the following mystical condition:

> A condition of complete simplicity
> (Costing not less than everything)
> And all shall be well and
> All manner of thing shall be well
> … And the fire and the rose are one.

So, after the fire of suffering, complete simplicity costs us 'not less than everything'. And then all shall be well. The inner peace of the Kingdom of God is coming. The Fire and the Rose – divine wrath and mercy – become one.

Accepting this may be important for our journey too. Dear spiritual friend, if you are passing through fire, may some of these words become a comfort to you on your way through this. It is a heat that often feels impossible. Perhaps it is nonetheless possible to hold on in it to the fact that in the end, all shall be well.

The Union of Fire and Love

The reality of the wound of Love coming with the Fire of God is in my view probably a test of its authenticity. Many so-called 'fiery encounters' may be described in different mystical or Pentecostal accounts. But without the wound, particularly the repentance and the completely new life that ensues, we may question their authenticity. Following this Fire experience and the ensuing wound, Richard Rolle goes on to speak of Divine Union coming with it:

> [The believer] forgets himself and everything else for Christ's sake; and so he says, 'Set me as a seal upon your heart' [Songs 8.6]. For what is love but the transforming of the desire into the loved thing itself? Or if you prefer, love is a great longing for what is beautiful, and good, and lovely, with its thought ever reaching out to the object of its love. And when he has got it a man rejoices, for joy is caused only by love. Every lover is assimilated to his beloved: love makes the loving one like what he loves.[210]

So it is that the fire-filled person draws near to Union. To use the image of St John of the Cross, like the dark wood thrown into the fire – the wood that becomes white hot and is consumed in the flame – so the heated-up believer approaches Union with God. Rolle puts it thus:

> It is the nature of love to melt the heart (as, for example, 'My soul melted when my Beloved spoke' [Songs 5.6]). For sweet love and a devout heart so dissolve in the divine sweetness that the will of man is united with the will of God in a remarkable friendship. In this union there is poured into the loving soul such sweetness of warmth, delight, and song that he who experiences it is quite unable to describe it.[211]

So after the fire, after the wound, after the suffering, may there be 'sweetness of warmth, delight ... and song'.

© Peronel Barnes, Chaoticorder

In the chaos of Peronel's striking stormy weather we sense the beauty.
It is as if there is Fire on the water – as is appropriate when we consider
that both are signs of the Holy Spirit – rushing winds and tongues of fire.

2

Later Stories of Fire

In the winter, seeing a tree stripped of its leaves and considering that within a little time the leaves would be renewed, he received such a high view of the providence and Power of God ... This view set him perfectly loose from the world and kindled in him such a love for God that he could not tell whether it had increased in the above forty years that he had lived since.
(Beaufort, his biographer, describing Brother Lawrence's Practice of the Presence of God)[212]

I was taken up in the love of God, so that I could not but admire the greatness of his love; and ... it was opened unto me by the eternal light and power, and therein I saw all that was done and to be done in Christ ... The Lord opened to me ... an infinite ocean of light and love which flowed ... Now that I was come up in spirit through the flaming sword into the paradise of God.
(George Fox's Journal)[213]

If we question the reality of Rolle's experience, it may be because we don't know it for ourselves. But in fact such a reality is relatively common in the mystical journeys of saints and leaders of old – and, I will suggest, in more recent Pentecostal encounters.

One of the most famous is that of the philosopher and mathematician Blaise Pascal, who recorded his own encounter with God. Pascal was the foremost mathematician of his day, discovering that vacuums are real and inventing the first digital calculator. He also wrote his great apologia for the Christian faith – his 'Pensées', in which we read: 'When I consider the short duration of my life, swallowed up in the eternity before and after, the little space which I fill, and even can see, engulfed in the infinite immensity of spaces of which I am ignorant ... *The eternal silence of these infinite spaces frightens me.*'

Later, Pascal the seeker after God had an experience of the Fire of God that had such an impression on him that he wrote down his 'Testament' and sewed it into the jacket found on him when he died at the young age of 39.

> The year of grace 1654
> Monday, 23 November, feast of St. Clement, pope and martyr, and others ...
> From about half past ten at night until about half past midnight, FIRE.
> God of Abraham, God of Isaac, God of Jacob
> not of the philosophers and of the learned.
> Certitude. Certitude.
> Feeling. Joy. Peace.
> God of Jesus Christ.
> My God and your God.
> Your GOD will be my God.
> Forgetfulness of the world and of everything, except GOD.
> He is only found by the ways taught in the Gospel.
> Grandeur of the human soul.
> Righteous Father, the world has not known you, but I have known you.[214]

Evelyn Underhill frequently returns to this moment in her magisterial 500-page analysis: *Mysticism*. She says:

> I know of few things in the history of mysticism at once more convincing, more poignant than this hidden talisman in which the brilliant scholar, the merciless disputant, has jotted down in ... words charged with passion – the inarticulate language of love – a memorial of the certitude, the peace, the joy above all ... which accompanied his apprehension of God.[215]

Dear spiritual friend, it is good to ask if you are open to understanding this, desiring this and, God willing, experiencing this today. The subject is mysterious but not uncommon.

Pascal's 'Memorial' continues by describing flashes of inspiration: joy; renunciation; submission total and sweet; eternal life and the knowledge of God. We pause to linger over these well-known words, and maybe to allow into ourselves the longing for such an encounter:

Joy, joy, joy, tears of joy.
I have departed from him:
They have forsaken me, the fount of living water.
My God, will you leave me?
Let me not be separated from him forever.
This is eternal life, that they know you, the one true God, and the one that you sent, Jesus Christ.
Jesus Christ.
Jesus Christ.
I left him; I fled him, renounced, crucified.
Let me never be separated from him.
He is only kept securely by the ways taught in the Gospel:
Renunciation, total and sweet.
Complete submission to Jesus Christ and to my director.
Eternally in joy for a day's exercise on the earth.[216]

It is worth mentioning that the brilliant architect of doctrine Thomas Aquinas, whose five-volume *Summa Theologica* has determined so much theological thinking, had a similar experience towards the end of his life. In 1273 he had a revelation that so affected him that he never wrote or dictated again, leaving his great work unfinished. When asked by his secretary to relent he replied: 'The end of my labours has come. All I have written appears to me as so much straw after the things that have been revealed to me.' He died three months later. Maybe Pascal felt the same. Sadly, no record has come to us of the content of Aquinas' encounter in the Fire of Love apart from its effect on him.

Another to experience this 'Fire of Love' was George Fox (1624–91). Early in his journal, he writes:

> One day when I had been walking solitary and come home, I was taken up in the love of God, so that I could not but admire the greatness of his love; and while I was in that condition, it was opened unto me by the eternal light and power, and therein I saw all that was done and to be done in Christ ... and my belief was in him. I saw that there was an ocean of darkness and death, but an infinite ocean of light and love which flowed over the ocean of darkness. In that I also saw the infinite love of God and I had great openings. Then came people from far and near to see me.[217]

People did indeed come from far and near. Perhaps it was his common touch, understanding, as he put it, 'that opening from the Lord – that to be bred at Oxford or Cambridge was not sufficient to fit a man to be a minister of Christ'. Fox was persecuted and imprisoned again and again for anti-clerical views like this, sometimes for months on end, always leading people in prison to faith. He was radical in his promotion of the role of women, his love and attention to indigenous peoples in the Americas, and to peace. In many ways he lived before his time. Despite divisions and persecutions, his following did not cease to grow until the eventual foundation of the Society of Friends, the Quakers, and all the reconciling peace movements that have flowed from them. All of the above arguably came from this 'inner light' and revelation granted to the great George Fox.

There are many stories of fiery encounter from the eighteenth-century times of Revival in Britain and America. John Wesley famously wrote: 'I felt my heart strangely warmed.' We might say that, thanks to Wesley, Whitefield, Wilberforce and others, Britain was visited by Revival, a complete 'Reformation of Manners', including the outlawing of the Slave Trade, and avoided the Terror of the Revolution that was taking place across the water in France. The warmth always invaded Wesley's preaching so that, as we have said, when asked what it was about his preaching that drew people from miles around in their thousands to hear him, Wesley famously replied: 'I set myself on fire and people come to watch me burn.'

One of the most articulate stories from this period is that of Sarah Edwards. She was the wife of Jonathan, future president of Princeton, who in his careful leadership documented the phenomena he observed in what became known as the Great Awakening. He asked her to write a careful account of the mystical things that had happened to her. Here is her account from Northampton, Massachusetts:

> That night, which was Thursday night, January 28, 1742 was the sweetest night I ever had in my life … I seemed to myself to perceive a glow of divine love come down from the heart of Christ in heaven, into my heart, in a constant stream, like a stream or pencil of sweet light. At the same time, my heart and soul all flowed out in love to Christ; so that there seemed to be a constant flowing and reflowing of heavenly and divine love, from Christ's heart to mine; and I appeared to myself to float or swim in these bright, sweet beams of the love of Christ, like the motes swimming in the beams of the sun or the streams of his light which come in at the window. So far as I am capable of making a comparison, I think that what I felt each minute, during the continuance

of the whole time, was worth more than all the outward comfort and pleasure which I had enjoyed in my whole life put together. It was a pure delight which fed and satisfied the soul. It was *pleasure*, without the least sting or any interruption. It was a *sweetness* which my soul was lost in. It seemed to be all that my feeble frame could sustain, of that fulness of joy which is felt by those who behold the face of Christ and share his love in the heavenly world ... I never felt such an entire emptiness of self-love or any regard to any private, selfish interest of my own. It seemed to me that I had entirely done with myself. I felt that the opinions of the world concerning me were nothing. The glory of God seemed to be all, and in all, and to swallow up every wish and desire of my heart.[218]

Jonathan Edwards' careful analysis of what we might call the 'phenomena of fire' neither condemned nor encouraged outward manifestations, swooning in meetings or whatever might and did occur (as it had done in the lives of the mystics). He above all tried to capture and lay hold on what for him was the greatest emphasis – the glory of God. He felt that people can seek to know the majesty of God, the sovereignty of God and then, if God wills, feel a sense of awe and of wonder. This is the impression Jonathan Edwards always conveys and creates. He taught that these things are possible for the humblest Christian. He was preaching and ministering mostly to ordinary people, and told them that these things are possible for all of them.

This is what we will rediscover in more recent accounts as people encounter the fire of love before Pentecostalism and at the moment of its birth. Forerunners of Pentecostalism included masterly preachers in the nineteenth century. One was Charles Finney, a prosecuting lawyer who had such a fiery mystical experience of encounter or Union that he immediately gave up his law career, saying to a would-be client: 'I have a retainer from the Lord Jesus Christ to plead his cause: I cannot plead yours.' In the following account of this encounter Finney explains what happened to him in 1821:

Without any expectation of it, without ever having the thought in my mind that there was any such thing for me, without any recollection that I had ever heard the thing mentioned by any person in the world, the Holy Spirit descended upon me in a manner that seemed to go through me, body and soul. I could feel the impression, like a wave of electricity, going through and through me. Indeed, it seemed to come in waves and waves of liquid love; for I could not express it in any other way. It seemed like the very breath of God. I can recollect distinctly that it seemed to fan me, like immense wings! No words can express the wonderful love that was shed abroad in my heart.[219]

In a different age completely to medieval, mystical times: the nineteenth century, and in a different place than Europe: the New World, people are seeking God. This time, as well as seeking holiness and union, they are looking for power to serve God. Mindful perhaps of Jesus' promise: 'You will receive power when the Holy Spirit comes upon you and you will be my witnesses', there is a longing for power for service, in this case preaching.

This fire, love, breath and wind of God of which Finney speaks are, as we have seen, true mystical signs in medieval times, but they also point forward to Azusa Street in 1906 and all the ensuing Pentecostal phenomena.

Many of these experiences are similar to those we have been discussing. There is a forsaking of the world, there is a lovesickness, and there is fruitfulness. Often there is a physicality, heat or fire – an embodiment that is equally concrete, surprising but also winsome.

Finney was a preacher who held his audience in rapt attention. In 1830–31, he led meetings in Rochester, New York. A pastor in New York who became a Christian in the Rochester meetings described them thus:

> The whole community was stirred. Religion was the topic of conversation in the house, in the shop, in the office and on the street. The only theatre in the city was converted into a livery stable; the only circus into a soap and candle factory. Drink shops were closed; the Sabbath was honoured ... a new impulse was given to every philanthropic enterprise; the fountains of benevolence were opened.[220]

I can't help being reminded of the famous arrival of Francis of Assisi in Bologna in August 1222. Here, at the news that Francis would preach, two thousand people ran to hear this 'troubadour of the King'. He spoke in the vernacular, which was unheard of, with vivid stories, accents and drama. And as he did, many were deeply affected as he 'preached penance' to the vast crowds. They found their lives changed as a result.

Charles Finney was also known for his innovations in preaching and the conduct of meetings, which often impacted entire communities. He had a deep insight into the almost interminable intricacies of human depravity. He is sometimes criticized (in my view, with reason) for what is perceived to be a kind of mechanical approach to his campaigns and for pressurizing his audiences. But in my view he introduced helpful and brave innovations of justice, including having women pray out loud in public meetings of mixed sexes. In addition to becoming a widely popular Christian evangelist, Finney was involved with social reforms, particularly the abolitionist movement. He frequently denounced slavery from the pulpit, calling it a 'great national sin', and refused Holy Communion to slaveholders. He became president of Oberlin College, the first American college to accept women and people of colour as students in addition to white men. From its early years, its faculty and students were active in the abolitionist movement, the 'Black Lives Matter' movement of its day. Like many mystics they were practical and well organized, participating together with people of the town in biracial efforts to help fugitive slaves on the Underground Railroad and to resist the Fugitive Slave Act of 1850.

In the days following the Day of Pentecost recorded in the Bible, we read that justice flowed like a river: the great and the lowly were touched and a redistribution of wealth occurred so that 'all the believers had everything in common. They sold their possessions and gave to any who had need' (Acts 2.45). In the days of the birth of Pentecostalism, we see a similar levelling and justice coming in the presence of 'the Fire of God'.

Sometimes, in my experience, people mimic received or observed behaviour in such gatherings. The work is turned into a 'system of conversion' quite foreign to Christianity. I admit the temptation is there – leading Underhill to speak disparagingly of what she calls 'revivalistic phenomena encouraged by American Protestantism' (we should add now 'encouraged by parts of the Church on every continent'). But at their best I would call the Pentecostal and Charismatic awakenings a new mystical movement ready to sweep across the world.

One of Underhill's definitions of true conversion is this: 'It is primarily an unselfing. The first birth of the individual is into his own little world. Conversion breaks in suddenly. The person emerges from a smaller limited world into a larger world of another kingdom. Their life becomes swallowed up in a larger whole.'[221] To use Jesus' words, the larger world is called the Kingdom of God. And we can't see it unless we are born from above (John 3.3).

We turn now to the mystical events of 1906. We shall see that, by this definition, the fire that was coming on the world was indeed part of 'true conversion'.

3

Fire of Love – Fire of Pentecost

It is interesting that there were almost identical sightings of fire in the time of St Francis of Assisi and at Azusa Street, Los Angeles, in 1906. Here is the account from Francis and Clare's friendship. Clare had often asked to meet to converse with Francis, whose disciple she was. For many understandable reasons Francis demurred until persuaded by his friends of the appropriateness of a meeting. Francis first prepared the meal and then he and others sat on the ground as was his custom, with Clare and other sisters. After the meal the conversation continued and Frances spoke with such inspiration that it seemed that time slowed and the presence of God was felt by those in the place. Brother Leo's 'Little Flowers of St Francis' (fourteenth century) describes what happened next:

> Whilst they were thus rapt, with eyes and hearts raised to heaven, the people of Assisi, and all the country round about, saw St Mary of the Angels as it were on fire, with the convent and the woods adjoining. It seemed to them as if the church, the convent, and the woods were all enveloped in flames; and the inhabitants of Assisi hastened with great speed to put out the fire. On arriving at the convent, they found no fire; and entering within the gates they saw St Francis, St Clare, with all their companions, sitting round their humble meal, absorbed in contemplation; then knew they of a certainty, that what they had seen was a celestial fire, not a material one, which God miraculously had sent to bear witness to the divine flame of love which consumed the souls of those holy brethren and nuns; and they returned home with great consolation in their hearts.[222]

This is certainly one of the moments of 'strange and weird stuff' advocated by Tom Holland as not to be dismissed.

The Pentecostal Awakening

As I have said, this mysterious event has a more modern counterpart. A similar story is told of the Pentecostal Awakening beginning in Azusa Street, Los Angeles, in 1906. The oft-repeated fact is that eyewitnesses on the street reported seeing a glow emanating from the building and heard sounds that were similar to explosions coming out of it. On more than one occasion the fire department came to the mission building because fire was seen rising from it. However, upon arrival, it was found that there was no natural fire.[223]

Rather, what was happening was metanoia, deep change, transformation. It was an experience like that of Francis and his companions – of hearing people 'speak of God so sweetly, so sublimely, and in a manner so wonderful' that it felt like Fire.

The background to this great mystical event was as follows. William Seymour, a 34-year-old African American, son of a former slave, was waiting on God with others, praying together in a poor area of Los Angeles, 'when suddenly, as though hit by a bolt of lightning fire, they were knocked from their chairs to the floor' and he and the other seven men began to speak in tongues and shout out loud in worship of God. The news spread; the city was stirred; crowds gathered; services were moved outside to accommodate the crowds who came from all around; people fell down as they approached and attributed it to God.

Stanley Frodsham quotes eyewitness descriptions of the scene: among first-hand accounts were reports of the blind having their sight restored, diseases cured instantly, and 'immigrants speaking in German, Yiddish, and Spanish all being spoken to in their native language by uneducated black members, who translated the languages into English by "supernatural ability'.[224]

The first edition of the journal *Apostolic Faith* claimed a common reaction to the revival from visitors. Proud, well-dressed preachers came to 'investigate'. 'Soon their high looks were replaced with wonder, then conviction comes, and very often you will find them in a short time on the dirty floor, asking God to forgive them and make them as little children.' The participants were criticized by some secular media and Christian theologians for behaviour considered to be outrageous and unorthodox, especially at the time. Long times of 'tarrying' and waiting on God and longing for him had led a tiny group into an experience of Visitation: the love of God was felt and experienced in a way that was fiery and far reaching.

We may find these 'strange and weird' events hard to believe or we may retain some scepticism. Speaking in tongues is a mystery – though such a feature of the earliest history of the Church as recorded in the book of Acts. It may help to see it as an intimate healing Love Language between a person and God ... admittedly strange, but not to be despised. As the apostle Paul said: 'I want you all to speak in tongues – but even more to prophesy' (1 Cor. 14.5). At any rate, the fact is also that this Pentecostal fire at Azusa Street – like the fire within Francis – spread throughout the world. We may think Azusa Street is nothing compared to the influence of Francis through the ages. But the truth is that from unlikely, unruly beginnings and phenomena such as speaking in tongues and people falling to the ground – being overwhelmed by 'the weight of glory' – extraordinary fruit in terms of justice and mission was the result.

First, there was the breaking down of the colour line – this was one reason the movement was so opposed as unseemly. Then it was a movement among the poor. People from a diversity of backgrounds came together to worship: men, women, children, black, white, Asian, Native American, immigrants, rich, poor, illiterate and educated. People of all ages flocked to Los Angeles with both scepticism and a desire to participate. The intermingling of races and then the group's encouragement of women in leadership was remarkable, as 1906 was still the height of the era of racial segregation in America, and it was still fourteen years prior to women having the right to vote in the United States. There was the erasing of the colour bar, the poverty line and some of the gender injustices of the day.

Finally, there was the spread of the movement: Many existing denominations adopted the fire of the Pentecostal message and experience. New denominations were born, such as the Assemblies of God in 1914 and the Pentecostal Church of God in 1919. This experience of 'Fire' at the Azusa Street Revival is regarded as the beginning of the modern-day Pentecostal Movement.[225] And of course, aspects of Pentecostal longing and experience spread in the Historic Churches through the charismatic movement. Today there are more than 600 million Pentecostal and charismatic believers across the globe, and this movement – unlike so many parts of the Church – is still growing today.

Charismystics

We might argue and say that the Pentecostal Movement began with a great deal of noise. But eyewitness accounts record long times of silence – crackling with expectancy maybe, but also silent longing. Where this is present and combines with Vision and Fire, I feel the link with mystics to such a degree that I sometimes use the term 'charismystic' to describe a contemporary phenomenon. Maybe I want the best of both worlds: silence, recollection, quiet, as well as union, visitation, fire. In my view there is a similarity between Pentecostal Revival phenomena and the intensity and intimacy experienced by many mystics. It is as if the mystics' longing for 'oneness', for union, and for connection with God is close to the longing to be 'filled with God's fullness' present in Azusa Street and other Pentecostal awakenings.

Pentecostal revival, including the Methodist Revival and the Welsh Revival of 1905–6 and the Pentecostal Awakening at Azusa Street, tell similar stories to those of the mystics we have been following but for more people at a time! It is a more widespread experience. In the Old Testament 'Fire' and Visionary Encounter were the experience of a very small number of people – and famous people at that. And then on the Day of Pentecost and in the early days of the Church the democratizing Spirit is poured out on both men and women, servants and free – even on Gentiles in Cornelius' house, as Peter says to those with him: 'Surely no one can prevent these people being baptized since they have received the Holy Spirit just as we have' (Acts 10.47).

In a similar way, while the mystical gift was received by comparatively few and those often famous saints and mystics in medieval history, here at Azusa Street, and in its forerunners, there comes a real levelling up.

Writing for another audience and with a concern to advocate that for Mystical experience to be real it must *work* for radical social justice, Dorothy Soelle wrote her brilliant, provocative work *The Silent Cry*, saying also:

> My most important concern is to democratise mysticism. What I mean to do is to re-open the door to the mystic sensibility, that's within all of us, to dig it out from under the debris of trivia from itself, trivialisation if you like.
>
> We're all mystics! That sentence contains in itself the right of every human being to beauty and vision. Is there such a thing as a human right to behold God?[226]

4

Fire and Love Today

Over the years, to speak personally, I have known growing times of silence in God's presence as well as the experience of absence of God and the Cloud of Unknowing. I have walked through different times of darkness, of suffering and of night. I guess in a way these are also the Fire – in the sense of the fire of suffering or refining.

But I believe that in the journey of desire for God I have also known this mystical fire and the joy of empowering encounter. I have also observed and heard about it in others. I wrote to a former student at Oxford, then intern and staff member at the church where I served in Oxford for nearly 20 years, and asked if she might write out her own story of the experience of Fire. To make this bridge between these worlds, I include here quite a long extract from her description of this experience. She writes:

> A few weeks into joining the school of ministry programme, our church was hosting a day conference called 'God's empowering presence.' Leading up to that day, I had a growing hunger to know more of God, I had been praying for some time, 'God use me and mould me into who you want me to be.'
>
> As the day began and from the moment people began to speak ... my heart was being stirred and it felt like it was being set on fire. Then as we began to sing songs of worship, my hands were shaking and ... It felt like there was a heavy weight on me. I had never experienced what I felt was the presence of God in such a tangible way before.
>
> During the teaching it was like there was electricity inside me, my lips were also tingling and felt like they were on fire. Later, I felt like I was being drenched by God in his love. I had such a deep sense of his holiness and power. Someone prayed for me who didn't know anything about me ... that I didn't need to carry around the cloak of my old reputation, to be free to live out my new life in Christ, also about my life being like a spring that Jesus' love would flow in and through to others and into the life of my family.

After the morning session I didn't really know what to do with myself so I went to be alone in our intern house. I felt like I needed to kneel before God and ask him what was going on … I was so aware in that moment of a feeling of freedom and delight in God. Looking back at the moment – it felt in some ways like a commission from God to send me out to serve in Oxford. As the day went on, I knew of some friends who were in the town centre on Broad Street. They were singing worship songs and offering to pray and chat with people. (Not something I would have ever felt particularly comfortable doing before!) I found myself going to meet them. That same sense of being overwhelmed by God's love, his fire in my heart that I had experienced in church was with me, like an equipping of boldness and freedom. As I joined in, a friend from Uni walked past. She was slightly confused by what I was doing but we ended up having a great chat and she came along to Church after that.

After that day I began to really experience more and more of the love and intimacy of God in a very tangible way, it was quite an intense season of learning to hear his voice in the secret place and through his word. Stepping out in prophetic gifts and seeing the Holy Spirit at work, a longing to share the love of Jesus with people and by his grace a desire to surrender my life more fully to him.

After then being led by God into further training and ministry among students in Oxford, there have been other times where I've had powerful moments of experiencing God's presence, particularly the weight of his glory and sense of burning fire in my heart, often during times of worship and prayer or when I've been involved in leading times of ministry in Church.

I've continued to know a growing deeper sense of his love and nearness that I believe came from encountering him on that day, but perhaps less like sparks and electricity and more like burning coals (that may be due right now to sleep deprivation of being a new mum …). I think like any relationship that grows there is a new depth of intimacy as you journey through ups and downs of life together, but I thank God for his kindness and unrelenting pursuit of love towards us in always desiring for us to know more of him.[227]

There are several things to notice here in this personal story.

Particularly, there is prior 'growing hunger' and desire. As so often, desire is the key. Augustine sums this up: 'The entire life of a good Christian is in fact an exercise of holy desire. You do not yet see what you long for, but the very act of desiring prepares you, so that when he comes you may see and be utterly satisfied.' And if you are someone who still hasn't found what you're looking for from God in terms of fire and filling, Augustine has this word of encouragement to keep desiring: 'God, by deferring our hope, stretches our desire, by desiring stretches the mind, by stretching makes it more capacious. Let us desire therefore, for we shall be filled.'[228]

François Fénelon puts it like this: 'He who desires not from the depths of his heart makes a deceptive prayer.'[229]

Then there is the very experience of: 'fire, weight, and electricity'. I want to stress that this is not of course essential to a walk with God into his mysterious presence. But it is worth noting that it *can* happen. It is a not-too-infrequent experience common to seekers after God. It is in my view not to be despised, but maybe rather sought after. At least God and his presence are to be longed for. It is founded, as we have seen, on Jesus' promise to his followers of being 'clothed with power from on high', fulfilled on the day of Pentecost when 'tongues of fire' were seen to be resting on the disciples. We have noted this testimony in Richard Rolle back in the 1300s, in Francis and Clare's meeting a hundred years before, in *The Cloud of Unknowing*'s 'Sparks of Fire' and John of the Cross's 'severe burn'. We see it in Pascal's mystical 'testament'. I think he would have spoken in terms of electricity had it been invented in the way we know it today! These experiences of Power continue through eighteenth- and nineteenth-century Revival phenomena down to the breaking out of the Pentecostal movement at the start of the last century and on into the present day.

Finally, there is fruit. Jesus said 'You will receive power when the Holy Spirit comes on you and you will be my witnesses'. In the contemporary personal story above, the experience is followed by the fruit of 'being a witness' to others of the truth of the gospel and this flowed into a fruitful discipling, pastoring and teaching role during the decade since these events. In my view this is an important mark of authenticity.

Beware of Imitations

I return now to what Evelyn Underhill, already quoted above, has disparagingly called 'revivalistic phenomena encouraged by American Protestantism'.[230] I repeat that of course we should sadly say: not only

American but everywhere ... She contrasts these with real conversion, which is indeed mystical awakening.

As I have said, I believe that such experiences of fire can be imitated, induced or reproduced falsely. They can be made to appear transactional: there can be an encouragement to 'come to Christ and be saved', or to 'come and be filled now with the Holy Spirit and Fire', which may appear too simple.

I believe an invitation to follow Christ should be given often or always in churches and gatherings. In many churches it is almost never given, which misses the mark and leaves people thirsting for God's living water. But where an invitation is given, I would rather hear it go deep: 'Believe in Christ as a child – in complete simplicity, a condition costing not less than everything.' Or 'Come to Christ, desiring to know the Holy Spirit's fire which will consume and transform you as well as empower.'

I believe there is false fire and real fire. False fire may include imitated behaviour. Real fire from God will include desire, deep repentance, metanoia and a complete change of life. The mystical way is deeper and more transformative by far. They may both be present in the same movement or even in the same meeting.

We may sadly say about these possible imitations, 'it was ever thus'. Already in Acts 8 Simon the magician saw the work of the Holy Spirit and was so impressed that he offered the apostles money to be able to confer the gifts of the Holy Spirit. He was roundly rebuked by Peter as being 'full of bitterness and captive to sin' (Acts 8.23). We may see hints of this still today in some church movements or systems of power, rather than holiness and sacrifice. We may easily see this in some TV ministries and heretical versions of Pentecostalism, including the tragic invention of the prosperity gospel which has overrun parts of Africa, Asia, America and now Europe and beyond, doing almost irreparable damage as false versions of Christianity can. We may also have seen leaders over-reaching and falling and causing great damage to people.

We may find these false fires so distasteful, anti-Christian even, that we run away for ever from outward expressions of joy or power in our faith. But if we are a sceptic concerning 'fire' today, this may be as much due to our own experience of suffering and pain and disappointment as well as the faults of such movements. If so, beware of missing true warming of the heart in your life. In the past people have condemned any expression of Christianity that contained superficial reproductions of behaviour. For example, years ago an easy target was to talk disdainfully about 'happy clappy Christianity'. The disdain came I think from the un-British expression of happiness in church – particularly if pressurized into this. I want to say I absolutely and entirely agree – almost. I agree about not being pressured into imitated behaviour. But I don't agree about not admitting the happiness – or the joy – into the church community, provided there is also lament and that suffering is acknowledged and incorporated into the communal life. Perhaps it is the monochrome or controlled version of church community which is a sign of heresy.

At any rate, what I see is that we risk throwing the baby (of Fire) out with the bathwater (of abuse or imitation – which extinguishes it anyway). Ever since the aberration of Simon Magus, we must be aware of abuse and avoid it. But the response to abuse should not be disuse but 'right use'.

The fact is, versions of Christianity which ridicule or banish or put out the Fire may be equally heretical. As I have said in the introduction, Tom Holland has helpfully called for Christianity not just to recycle 'soft-left liberal versions of Jesus being a nice guy', but to remember that in fact 'Christians believe that the whole fabric of the cosmos was ruptured by this strange singularity of someone who is a God and a man setting everything on its head – and – to say it is supernatural is to downplay it'!

Holland adds: 'if you don't believe that, you are not really a confessional Christian. So if you believe that, it should be possible to dwell on the other strange and weird stuff that comes as part of the Christian package.'[231]

It is in this same vein that I believe we may see these 'strange' experiences of Fire as 'wonderful signs'. I plead for us to see them as part of our mystical Christian inheritance, just as much as silent longing in the Cloud. They go alongside the journey through the Dark Night. They may come after or before. In the case of Jesus, his experience of baptism and the voice of affirmation from heaven was followed by a dark night of 40 days in the desert. The landscapes of Cloud, Night, Fire and Song I am charting come to us in different orders and maybe repeating at different times. I believe that all are part of our journey.

And to reach the end of this roadmap, we turn now to 'The Song'.

PART 4

The Song

© *Peronel Barnes, 'Risingabove'*

Rising above the stormy landscape, the fire of the sun changes everything. Water and waves turn golden and the land emerges sharply. Everything is illuminated by fire. In our spiritual journey, fire changes everything too. Perspective lengthens and we see details which were shrouded in darkness.

Colours emerge and hope comes for the future. Above all we can simply enjoy and be still before the landscape. And sit before the warming fire of God's love.

I

A Brief History of Song

It seems wrong that out of this bird,
Black, bold, a suggestion of dark
Places about it, there yet should come
Such rich music ...
(R. S. Thomas, 'A Blackbird Singing')[232]

And as he went, he sang ...
(John Bunyan, *The Pilgrim's Progress*)

Praise for the singing,
Praise for the morning,
...
Born of the one light
Eden saw play;
Praise with elation,
Praise every morning
God's recreation
Of the new day!
(Eleanor Farjeon, 'Morning has Broken')[233]

At the heart of the book of books, in the middle of the Bible, stands the Song of Songs.

At the end of the Bible there is a New Song unceasingly sung. That is our future in heaven.

Creation also begins, it seems, in Song.

In the Bible, Job is told that at the dawn of time, 'the morning stars sang together' (Job 38.7).

Perhaps it is because of this that C. S. Lewis's Narnia and J. R. R. Tolkien's Middle Earth are formed in song and music. Narnia begins in singing which seems 'to come from all directions at once'. It has no words and no clear tune, but for the protagonist it is 'so beautiful he could hardly bear it'. Tolkien's creation story begins with the Creator speaking: 'Behold your music!' And the Music of the Ainur, at the start of his *Silmarillion*, creates worlds.[234]

So, at the beginning, at the end and at the heart of God's Creation, we find music, At the mid-point of the Bible, there is not only the poetic, mystical Song of Songs, but also the Psalms. It seems our destiny is to join in with this Song. After the Cloud, the Night and the Fire, I include it as the fourth landscape for our journey on earth and then throughout eternity. It seems we do well to understand and receive and sing a Song in this life.

The state of love, said Richard Rolle, is the state of Sweetness and Song – 'the welling up of glad music in the simple soul', a person's natural expression of a joy which surpasses our powers to describe with mere words. When we come to the mystics, 'songs of lovely loving commonly burst up – What are the servants of God but his minstrels?' asks St Francis, for whom to sing seemed to him to be his spiritual function. John of the Cross wrote songs of love to his Love. Teresa of Avila made rustic hymns and carols in the local dialect for her sisters to enjoy.[235]

When we say someone is 'on song' in the sports world, it means for them to be at their sweet spot and playing well. In a deeper way, our quest in this book has been to be 'on song' through the different landscapes of life. For the mystical mind, this means to learn to live life as a lover of God and to position ourselves to experience his love. It may be that you can't sing in tune, but I am speaking metaphorically. It can be the 'silent song' that you favour or a more outward version.

Dear spiritual friend, as we journey through valleys and depths as well as the heights, the question to ask is: how might our whole life come back to its first love and become 'on song'? This is the subject of this fourth and final stretch which I will explore. But first, here is a bit of background.

Songs are all around us – on TV and social media as well as filling every public space. And we do naturally sing, I believe. But it is equally true that singing can be extinguished in our lives. I have found that in times of trouble I have stopped singing. Sometimes I have stopped praying too. Silence has been my last resort. In a marriage, losing communication and intimacy may be a sign of deep fissures in relationship in which case great care is needed if there is to be recovery. But sometimes communication is lost through forgetfulness, busyness, the invasive changes of the life stage we find ourselves in. Sometimes communication and intimacy can be restored by a coming to our senses and re-establishing our first love. In a similar way with our song to God, it may be that we can recover it by learning to sing again first as a spiritual discipline and as a heart response, and then we may soon find we are indeed 'on song' again.

The beneficial physiological effects of singing on mood, outlook and general health are well-documented. Researchers are discovering that singing is the perfect tranquillizer – the kind that both soothes your nerves and elevates your spirits. The elation may come from endorphins or oxytocin: both are hormones released by singing. Oxytocin alleviates anxiety and stress and enhances feelings of trust and bonding, which may explain why still other studies have found that singing lessens feelings of depression and loneliness.[236]

Apparently the hills are capable of singing together for joy (Psalm 98.8), the trees can sing (Isa. 14.4) as well as the morning stars (Job 38.7). It is not *just* the birds that sing, but they evidently do sing. Gerard Manley Hopkins wrote of the effect of their song:

Nothing is so beautiful as Spring –
   When weeds, in wheels, shoot long and lovely and lush;
   ... and thrush
Through the echoing timber does so rinse and wring
The ear, it strikes like lightnings to hear him sing.[237]

This 'lightning strike' of singing is intriguing. Why is this? Is it because there is something vulnerable about singing in that the inner voice is heard in it? One good spiritual exercise for creativity is to compose your own song. It is challenging but can be healing and restorative to see if you can cultivate a season of singing in your own life. Sometimes singing is a response to hope: 'Sing O barren woman, break forth into song,' says the prophet (Isa. 64.1), and we can do this even in times of pain and darkness. As we do so, we will find the healing power of Song.

Then there is the community that is built through song – for in the Bible songs are written to be sung in community.

I once prepared an order of service for a church wedding with a future bride who asked me: 'Do we have to sing – why would we sing together?', adding that they did not know any hymns anyway and nor would their friends. It was a good question – of course you do not *have* to sing at a wedding – and it made me reflect. I don't know if I said all this, but I found myself thinking that it was a chance for people to declare something together 'with one voice', in unison. It might help their friendship community to find its expression – and love deepens when it is expressed. Further, as I say, singing is quite a vulnerable act and so to dare to sing releases courage and commitment. I remember another bride saying to me after her wedding that 'it was the first time I had ever heard my husband sing' – and she liked the sound of it. So it was that for the first wedding the couple chose among three great hymns: 'Morning has Broken' – with its epic words reflecting on the sunlight, the morning, the one light in Eden and after imagining these springing fresh into the world, concluding:

Praise for the singing.

The wedding was a moving event – and, I daresay, even more so with the singing,

So, 'Praise for the singing ...'

Certainly, the worldwide church seems to have discovered this genius power of the Song, and I do believe it is our destiny to discover it together.

The first song in the Bible is the song of Moses and Miriam in Exodus 15. Many of the prophets recorded their songs and the greatest collection is of course the Psalms. Then we find Jesus who, on the night he was betrayed, found time to sing with his disciples (Matt. 26.30).

Singing has continued with different emphases and styles throughout the history of the Church. We are inspired by the fifth-century St Patrick's Breastplate ('I bind unto myself today the strong name of the Trinity'). This was a song of protection in a context of opposition. Then one of the first English singers was Caedman who in the sixth century, according to the eighth-century historian, Bede, learned to compose one night in the course of a dream. He later became an inspirational Christian poet. His most famous song is one celebrating God's creation:

> Now we shall honour heaven-kingdom's guardian,
> the measurer's might and his mind's plan,
> the work of the father of glory as he of each wonder,
> eternal lord, the origin established,
> He first created for the children of men
> heaven for a roof, holy creator.
> Then Middle-earth mankind's guardian,
> eternal Lord, after bestowed
> the lands to men Lord almighty.[238]

Caedmon shows the rich appreciation of Creation in a way that we would do well to recover in today's worship world!

Later the soaring plainsong of Hildegard of Bingen (b. 1098) was completely ground-breaking and was said to 'reflect the song of heaven' – in the same way as that the music of the sixteenth-century Thomas Tallis.

'Heaven was opened and a fiery light of exceeding brilliance came and permeated my whole brain and inflamed my whole heart and my whole breast,' Hildegard wrote. Her lack of formal training in Latin means her texts are not confined and the words flow straight out of her head like a sort of divine stream-of-consciousness. Introducing her to a Classic FM audience, Owen Hopkin wrote: 'For religious poetry it is almost indecent in its lushness. It abounds in colourful images of natural, organic things – gardens, growth, fecundity, flowers, jewels. Take this description of the Virgin Mary in Ave, Generosa, which recalls the imagery of the Bible's 'Song of Songs': 'Your flesh has known delight; like the grassland touched by dew and immersed in its freshness: so it was with you, O mother of all joy.'[239]

Hildegard's song-writing and music was of great intensity. Here is one example:

> O eternal God, now may it please you
> to burn in love
> So that we become the limbs
> fashioned in the love you felt
> when you begot your son
> at the first dawn
> before all creation ...[240]

That we might sing to God inviting him to burn in love – asking for the congregation to be united with him, becoming 'limbs fashioned in love' – seems to expect 'something' to occur in worship in our hearts. And this echoed later in history – for example in the music of Revival and Awakenings which, as we shall see, seeks to touch our hearts.

Frances of Assisi 'loved above all other birds "a certain little bird which is called the lark", famed for its song. His whole life was one long march to music through the world.'[241] His Canticle of the Sun is well known. Pope Francis' 2015 encyclical *Laudato Si* takes its name and inspiration from Saint Francis' work. The title means 'Praise Be to You' in medieval Italian, a phrase that is repeated throughout the Canticle.

In it Francis praises God (*Laudato Si*) through brother sun, sister moon, brother wind, sister water, brother fire, mother earth – and in the end concludes: 'Praised be You, my Lord, through our Sister Bodily Death, from whom no living man can escape.'

Other brilliant compositions of Francis translated into English as songs include: 'All creatures of our God and King' and 'Make me a channel of your peace'. These show the drift into song inevitable for those with a close awareness of God's presence.

Martin Luther wrote that 'next to the Word of God, the noble art of music is the greatest treasure in the world. It directs our thoughts, minds, hearts, and spirits'. He desired that 'all Christians would love and regard as worthy the lovely gift of music, which is a precious, worthy, and costly treasure given to mankind by God. The riches of music are so excellent and so precious that words fail me whenever I attempt to discuss and describe them.'[242] Luther was an artist, a musician, writing songs that for hundreds of years would be passionately sung by worshippers in their congregations.

John Calvin contributed in inestimable ways to protestant singing by publishing his 'Psalter' in 1543. In the Preface he wrote: 'We find that (music) has a sacred and almost incredible power to move hearts in one way or another ... to incite us to pray to and praise God, and to meditate upon his works in order to love, fear, honour and glorify him ...' He recommends learning the psalms by heart for the purpose of 'enjoying God': 'After the intelligence must follow the heart and the affection, a thing which is unable to be except if we have the hymn imprinted on our memory, in order never to cease from singing. For each one who desires to enjoy himself, does so honestly and according to God.'[243]

Noting music's 'almost incredible power to move hearts', Calvin is keen for the Christian to 'enjoy himself', 'never cease from singing'. These composers and so many others were concentrating on declaring the objective beauty of God, His creation, His deeds, and what they saw as the truth about salvation and God's protection – for example, Luther's 'A mighty stronghold is our God'.

But when the eighteenth-century Great Awakening occurred (itself an almost mystical moment), it fell to Charles Wesley to do something new. This was to regularly include emotion and the feelings of the singers in the lyrics of his great hymns. There had been hints of emotion in the past, for example in Bach's moving *Matthew Passion*. And Handel's equally brilliant *Messiah* is stirring, famously causing King George II – and audiences ever since – to stand for the Hallelujah Chorus. Its lyrics are exclusively selected Bible verses. But for Charles Wesley this is now done in a completely different way, which in fact leads those singing to encounter God, one might say again, in an almost mystical way. For example, 'And can it be?' has the dramatic lines:

> My chains fell off, my heart was free;
> I rose, went forth and followed Thee.
> ... Bold I approach the eternal throne,
> And claim the crown, through Christ my own.

Even the more measured 'Love divine, all loves excelling' is filled with emotions and longings on the part of the company of singers. The hymn continues:

> Visit us with Thy salvation;
> enter every trembling heart.

It is as if now, during the very singing, transformation and metanoia and what is almost mystical union may happen, as the next verse suggests:

> Breathe, O breathe Thy loving Spirit
> into every troubled breast!
> Let us all in Thee inherit,
> let us find the promised rest.
> Take away our love of sinning;
> Alpha and Omega be;
> end of faith, as its beginning,
> set our hearts at liberty.

This power of emotion and desire for encounter in song is, I believe, what the extraordinarily successful and popular 'Contemporary Worship Movement' has tapped into. Combined with a generation's identity which is arguably based on individual feelings and their emotions, this has proved revolutionary for the content of 'Song' before God today for parts of the Church on every continent.

Our cultural taste may be for contemporary or for classical. We may love the classical: Tallis or Taverner or Byrd or Bach. It may be Handel or Elgar or Rutter or Rachmaninov, or the greatest Song of Songs composer, Palestrina – to name but a very few who have created glorious, healing Song. I admit these are where I find my heart warmed.

By contrast, we may love contemporary worship. To move into another world, we may love Redman or Tomlin or Townend or Hughes. We may be moved by Bethel or Housefires, Elevation or Rend Collective. The latter names may be unfamiliar to some readers, but Matt Redman's '10,000 Reasons' song or hymn has been played at least 63 million times online and sold 6.3 million copies. It's believed that over 100 million people in the world have sung Getty and Tomlin's 'In Christ Alone'. These impressive numbers compare to the 1 million copies of sheet music sold of Rutter's 'Shepherd's Pipe Carol'.

It is only 60 years since A. W. Tozer wrote his small book *Worship: The Missing Jewel of the Evangelical Church*.[244] But since then there has been the Contemporary Worship Revolution. Since the advent of the internet, a great new worship song can fill countries and continents within weeks across the world like an online flood. The popularity of contemporary worship songs is staggering.

Contemporary worship songs do many things, but one is to draw the congregation into Union with God. One commentator observes: 'There is a collective "consciousness of an active God in the midst of his people". Gathered worship is the place where, "God's nearness has an extra reality".'

This emphasis on the immanence of God is captured in a statement by Vineyard theologian Don Williams: 'As worship ascends, God comes down. He becomes experienced as immanent.'[245]

I believe these are the inheritors of Charles Wesley's genius for touching and expressing emotion as well as desiring Union with Christ. Wesley was able to express deep, quite complex, careful spiritual truths alongside emotion, whereas many contemporary songs today tend to be more like soundbites or flashes of emotion: at best snatches of Truth, at worst what we might call 'all about me songs'.

This is the age we live in and so it is not surprising. Forty years ago, Alasdair MacInytre argued in *After Virtue* that in the cultural moment we now inhabit we are not governed by faith or reason but by 'emotivism'[246] (and now, one might add, by emojis). Not all contemporary worship is like this, of course. And I salute the endeavours of these often brilliant song writers. It is true, as I have said elsewhere, few songs have the density of Charles Wesley's carol 'Hark the Herald Angels Sing', with its informative as well as stirring lines:

late in time behold him come,
offspring of a virgin's womb!

> Veiled in flesh the Godhead see,
> hail, the incarnate Deity!

Today's best-loved songs are seldom so packed with content and therefore risk some loss of substance and truth. But their massive popularity reminds us of the power of the Song, our destiny.

Some contemporary worship songs succeed in bringing both truth and emotion into a few lines. One such is Andrew Peterson's 2018: 'Is He Worthy?'[247] We sang this epic lament/anthem at my sister-in-law's tender and tearful funeral after her tragic death in a traffic accident. We will speak again of the place of lament in song. But this one contains sadness, hope, rich salvation history, referencing Revelation 5, and a longing for the New Creation.

It begins: 'Do you feel the world is broken?' with the response: 'We do.' The song continues to ask: 'Do we feel creation groaning, the shadows deepen?' This draws the people in, admitting pain but affirming hope with hints at truths found in scripture. References of faith and anticipation continue throughout the song, evoking light in the darkness, the coming New Creation, the light and love of the Father, and whether there is anyone worthy to 'open the seals', and remembering the longed-for Lion of Judah. These are powerful, mysterious references, filled with content and, in my view, are consoling.

The ending echoes the title of the song: 'Is he worthy? Is he worthy?' And answers itself: 'He is! He is!' It shows again how emotion can link to content and truth and provide psalm-like song for today.

For our own 'Song', objective truth, perspective as well as personal resolve, the expression of loving commitment and the desire for Union are all important. There are many factors leading to the popularity of a song today. Being in touch with people's feelings, having a great voice, being known, having a platform, musicality and production are important, of course. I was once present at a Christian music and book event where the person behind producing and publishing the 2012 song '10,000 Reasons' received the Album of the Year award and I asked him what the secret of a great worship song was. He thought for a moment and replied: 'It must have memorable words, an anthemic tune, and someone dies and goes to heaven in the last verse!' Considering this, I realized it was indeed true of popular songs like 'Amazing Grace' (apparently the most recorded worship song), 'How Great Thou Art' and indeed '10,000 Reasons' itself. 'Amazing Grace' ends with a glimpse into heaven: 'When we've been there ten thousand years'; 'How Great

Thou Art' ends with 'When Christ shall come ... and take me home'; and 10,000 Reasons has: 'And on that day when my strength is failing, the end draws near, and my time has come.'

This is the eternal perspective of the new Creation (see also Wesley's 'Finish then thy new creation'). Perspective helps us to be 'on song', in this case giving us the perspective of eternity. The majestic song which is Psalm 23 is the great forerunner of this. Here the table spread before me with its overflowing cup comes only after the journey through the valley of the shadow of death.

By definition, the last scenes of the Bible itself have this element: In the book of Revelation, a new song is sung by every creature in the new creation where every tear is wiped away and the healing of the nations comes. Before that there has been the Cloud of Exodus, the Night of much of the Old Testament and between the testaments, the bright flaming Fire of Christ's presence on earth, and now, in the end eternally, the Song.

2

The Mingling of Joy and Lament and Community in Song

Although we were created with Song, and our DNA and destiny is to sing, I am aware that for some reading this it may be that suffering and sorrow or sickness have stopped up their song. But it is a comforting solace if even then another music emerges, despite our circumstances, perhaps like the gorgeous music of the Spirituals which came forth from times of slavery and suffering. Some titles are 'My Way's Cloudy', 'Hard Trial', 'Nobody Knows the Trouble I'm in', 'Sometimes I feel like a motherless child', 'I'm gonna lay down my heavy load down by the riverside'. They are all the richer for this context – and our song can be too.

In the Bible, in times of great disaster, personal violence and starvation, invasion and what even seemed like the brutal end of Israel, there emerged a new Song with a new name: 'Lament', which had its own book named after it, and which poetically described these things.

As we have seen. Lamentations was born out of real trouble, disappointment, disaster and death. And in life there will be real trouble, disappointment, disaster and death. It may not reach, please God, the devastating proportions of the holocaust described in the book of Lamentations, but for some it will. And for many there will be winter, night, desert and deep waters of death or depression poured over lives at different times and intensities.

Life contains some sadness and bereavement that can linger. Whether it is the loss of our spouse, a parent, a friend, a job, a place or a church, many Christians do not know how to grieve. The fact is that the evangelical wing of the Church (to which I owe my life), and the Church in general, are not too good at expressing this.

It may help to remember that as well as being the joy of man's desiring,[248] Jesus was a man of sorrows and acquainted with grief. And if we do fail to grieve, we can fall ill and become unhealthy: we are holistic beings whose bodies respond to our circumstances. Let us learn from

Jesus who, according to the book of Hebrews, during his life on earth 'offered up prayers and petitions with fervent cries and tears to the one who could save him from death, and ... was heard' (Heb. 5.7).

The Bible's book of songs, the Psalms, also allows space for Lament as well as for Joyful Praise songs and Rehearsals of God's great deeds. About a third of the Psalms are songs of sadness and protest. This is important in so many ways.

First, it gives language to sadness. This is good for our health and good for the emotional health of the whole Church. So many liturgies today are filled with joy and hope, leaving no room for truthful expressions of sadness or even despair. It seems we have to live in a perpetually upbeat mood if we are to be part of community. Yet I believe that this absence of sadness or sorrow will destroy true community in the end because it rings false and leads to weariness and hollow-sounding clashing cymbals.

It's worth noting that, in our culture, emotion in song is now routinely expressed in sometimes challengingly honest ways. As part of a recent summer tour, one of my granddaughters (aged 12) attended in person a Taylor Swift stadium concert (along with 4.35 million other people at 60 tour dates throughout the world). It was an emotional event to say the least. Taylor's genius, among many other things, is to know how to express sadness, emotion, raw disclosure and painful thoughts about breakup, as well as regret and nostalgia. She knows how to lament and so connects with her massive young audience worldwide. Of course, there is reorientation celebration and joy as well.

Part of the power of such stadium events is the entire crowd or community joining in Song. It is not usually a solo act or a performance with listeners but a huge 60,000 strong choir joining together as one in words people know by heart. We can see this by a glance at the British festival at Glastonbury, attended by around 100,000 people singing with Chris Martin of Coldplay the sad lyrics of 'Fix You', about grief around death.[249] The message is that when someone feels broken there are people who care and want to help them heal, but that this may feel like them trying to 'fix you'. This song does not necessarily have a happy ending: it is a lament. And there are many tears 'When you lose something you cannot replace.' The song is so well loved that as a result the emotional rescue embedded in it has turned stadiums into secular churches.

The fact is that true Christian Song will also include disorientation and lament. In his brilliant work commenting on and explaining the

THE MINGLING OF JOY AND LAMENT AND COMMUNITY IN SONG

psalms, Walter Brueggemann has spoken of their pattern of Orientation, Disorientation and Reorientation. Here he outlines more wide-ranging consequences if we ever lose the element of Disorientation and Lament in our Song:

> A community of faith that negates lament soon concludes that the hard issues of justice are improper questions to pose at the throne of God, because the throne seems only to be a place of praise. I believe it thus follows that if justice questions are improper questions at the throne ... they soon appear to be improper questions in public places, in schools, in hospitals, with the government and eventually even in the courts. Justice questions disappear ... the order of the day comes to seem absolute, beyond question, and we are left only with grim obedience and eventually despair. The point of access for serious change has been forfeited when the propriety of this speech form is denied.[250]

There is Lament, but after the disorientation and sadness in the psalms it is true to say that they move beyond the disorientating lament language to praise and declarations of the goodness of God who reorientates everything.

Richard Rolle is one whose entire life was reoriented when he experienced the Fire of Love. He understood the disruptive power of Song in all circumstances in the Fire of Love when, as we have seen, he wrote:

> This is the life of the perfect man – it means ... burning in love for the creator alone; experiencing, after the bitter sorrow, the sweetness of heavenly contemplation ... And thus to be taken hold of and pass through the joy of loving God to spiritual song – through contemplation to heavenly music ... to sit alone, that away from the racket, my song would flow more easily.[251]

Julian of Norwich tells how silent prayer itself is a 'marvellous melody of endless love':

> My understanding was lifted up into Heaven where I saw our Lord as a lord in his own house, who has called all his dear worthy servants and friends to a stately feast. ... I saw him royally reign in his house, full filling it with joy and mirth ... with marvellous melody of endless love, in his own fair blessed Countenance.[252]

Julian's *Revelations of Divine Love* still give counsel and comfort to the burdened and perplexed. Her fourteenth-century world was as marked by aggression, insecurity and change as ours is today. Her most famous words, born of extreme personal suffering, 'All shall be well and all manner of thing shall be well' are as needed now as when she wrote them. She writes elsewhere of hearing that 'the Good Lord said full blissfully: "Lo how that I loved thee – My Darling behold and see that is the Lord thy God that is thy Maker and thine endless joy and for thy love, rejoice thou with me' – see what endless bliss I have in thy salvation".'[253] And all this came with the revelation of the 'marvellous melody of endless praise' as her background music and her destiny in heaven.

She speaks of the struggle between life and death as 'the medley of human life – singing in counterpart through our days' with the 'Melody of his divine presence that never changes':

> This mingling of life and death, rising and falling is so strange ... On the one hand, we live in a holy agreement with God; when we feel the Divine Presence in our lives, we set our wills, our intellects, our souls, and our strength to following God. Then ... we fall once more into such darkness that we stumble into all manner of sorrows and troubles ... This is the medley of human life: faith and sorrow, insight and darkness, joy and agony, singing in counterpart through our days. But God wants us to know that through it all the Divine Presence is the melody that never changes.[254]

Another mystic, St Francis of Assisi, who had regularly called the birds together for worship, ended his life on earth singing. Thomas of Celano's 'First Life' records this:

> So after he had rested for a few days in the place he had so greatly longed for, and knew that the time of death was imminent, he called to him two brethren, his specially loved sons, and bade them in exultation of spirit sing with a loud voice praises to the Lord concerning death which was near, or rather life which was so close at hand; while himself, as he was able, broke into that Psalm of David, 'I cried unto the Lord with my voice, with my voice unto the Lord I made supplication.' (Psalm 142.1)[255]

St Francis is using the psalms for language and so can we. We can indeed learn them by heart and find in them a very present help in times of trouble.

Psalms have a freedom in the face of adversity. Praise is an act of basic trust. It is in fact helpful that a psalm may begin in hurt, rage, need, indignation, isolation and abandonment.[256] But they come back to Praise. The book of Psalms concludes with six songs of clear 'basic trust'. For Brueggemann, Psalm 145 is 'an evangelical act that invites a deep departure from the greed systems of self-securing'.[257] In my view this is vital for the mystical journey. To sing psalms corporately is an act of abandonment to divine providence and trust in God. This is not a denial of trouble but a decision to trust in God.

Praise is also an assault on idols: it is 'an essentially polemical act'.[258] We are not bowing down to Mammon or to any System or Empire or the Smartphone but exalting God alone. In this sense it is a political act too. Our joy, our happiness comes not from circumstances or from a change in government but from God!

When we are declaring by singing, this is equally radical. It doesn't matter if the singing is silent and in the heart or noisy. Somehow singing involves vulnerability and weakness and trust. This is why it often moves us – as well as its beauty. We are somehow moving to solidarity with creation, which is naturally filled with bird song (if we would or could but hear it). Jesus said: 'Consider the birds'. When we sing, we are in a way imitating them too, as Jesus instructed us – living carelessly and trustingly. We may also be joining with all creation in our ultimate love song to God in which we find connection and healing from all our ills.

3

Joining the Song of Songs

In the end, the Cloud, the Night and the Fire all lead to the Song. In all the cloudy apprehensions of God, the dark nights of absence, the fire of God's presence, I believe our destiny is to become part of what the Bible calls the Song of Songs. It is called this because it dares to speak of that for which we are created, namely to discover the Divine Romance.

Bernard de Clairvaux writes:

> But there is that other song which, by its unique dignity and sweetness, excels all those I have mentioned and any others there might be; hence by every right do I acclaim it as the Song of Songs. It stands at a point where all the others culminate. Only the touch of the Spirit can inspire a song like this, and only personal experience can unfold its meaning … It is a tune you will not hear in the streets, these notes do not sound where crowds assemble; only the singer hears it and the one to whom he sings – the lover and the beloved. It is preeminently a marriage song telling of the mutual exchange of the heart's affections.[259]

Bernard here is introducing one of the first of his 86 sermons on the Song and describing its pre-eminence. He is sometimes called a mystic and sometimes described as 'the last of the Fathers'.

He unites us to wells that have often been blocked up for today's Church.

Earlier in our journey, we have seen that *The Cloud of Unknowing* calls us to love, as opposed to knowledge … and the Song of Songs is a call to love God – hard to understand without entering through love:

> All rational beings contain two faculties, the power of knowing and the power of loving. To the intellect, God who made us is forever unknowable, but to the second, love, he is completely knowable. [260]

In a similar way, the Song of Songs may only be known through love.

This was the view of C. H. Spurgeon, who wrote: 'The Song is a golden casket, of which love is the key rather than learning.'

Spurgeon was arguably a mystic in the sense of valuing the nearness and dearness and mystery of God. He was also a prince among nineteenth-century preachers. In one of his 52 sermons on the Song, which gathered thousands in what was then the largest church in London, he gives this judgement on the Song:

> The Song occupies a sacred enclosure into which none may enter unprepared. 'Put off thy shoes from off thy feet, for the place whereon you stand is holy ground,' is the warning voice from its secret tabernacles.
>
> The historical books I may compare to the outer courts of the Temple; the Gospels, the Epistles and the Psalms, bring us into the holy place or the Court of the priests; but the Song of Solomon is the most holy place: the holy of holies, before which the veil still hangs to many an untaught believer ... The Song is a golden casket, of which love is the key rather than learning.[261]

Many of the songs of the Psalms are love songs: The strength of feeling often comes through as we are drawn into singing about God's *hesed* (his unfailing love): 'I love you Lord, my strength'; 'I love the house where you dwell'; 'In the morning I will sing of your love'; 'Let the morning bring me word of your unfailing love' (Psalms 18, 26, 59, 138).

But when we turn to the Song of Songs, we find an entire book devoted to a love affair between humankind and the Bridegroom.

Dear beloved reader, maybe an exercise now would be to pause and re-read the Song's eight chapters before continuing. Reading the Song from the point of view of the Bride and from the point of view of Love can be life-changing. I recommend reading the whole of the Song of Songs at least three times a year!

This book, which so nourished the Church Fathers and the medieval and contemporary mystics, has been one of my life's love affairs in all the Bible. It is a rich, deep well. I believe it describes at the human level the ebb and flow of an earthy love song between a betrothed woman and her Prince. At the same time, it is a brilliant allegory of humankind's Divine Romance with the Beloved. It describes humankind's alienation, illuminates the link between our sexuality and the Holy Longing and gives pathways to union and oneness with God.[262]

According to Karl Barth, 'The Song of Songs is one long description of the Rapture, the unquenchable yearning and the restless willingness and readiness with which both partners in this covenant hasten towards an encounter.'[263]

The Song held a central place of fascination for the Church Fathers as well as for so many mystics, including Teresa, Julian of Norwich, Hildegard of Bingen and Richard Rolle. We have seen its importance for St John of the Cross: all of his poetry and writings are in fact one long exposition of the Song of Songs. We have seen that his most famous poem of all, 'The Dark Night of the Soul', is a sparkling exploration of Song of Songs 3.

The mystics returned again and again to unblock more meaning from the Song. It was their background music. They interpreted it and worked it into their writing or made it the chief subject of their journey. We now dig deeper into this well which is the Song of Songs to identify ways that we can be refreshed, so that, like *The Pilgrim's Progress*, it might be said of us on our journey: *'and as he went, he sang.'*

Challenging Themes for Daily Living from the Song of Songs

'Let him kiss me with the kisses of his lips' is the opening desire of the Song. This is immediately intimate and, let us admit, challenging. If this is about the Divine Romance, then what does this mean? I believe the kisses of God have many meanings, but principally they refer first to the Incarnation, when God our Creator, the Holy One of Israel, entered our humanity to be born as a baby in a manger and to live and then die and then rise again from the dead. I would say that this was the divine Kiss of Life. To use the words of a famous hymn of the 1904 Welsh revival, this is 'when the prince of life our ransom / kissed a guilty world with love'.

A thousand years ago, Bernard de Clairvaux wrote of this:

> The mouth that kisses signifies the Word, who assumes human nature; the nature assumed receives the kiss; the kiss is none other than the one mediator between God and mankind, himself a man, Jesus Christ ... A fertile kiss then, a marvel of self-abasement that is not a mere pressing of mouth upon mouth; it is the uniting of God with man.[264]

For Origen it meant also the teachings of Christ – 'For the kisses of Christ are those that he bestowed on the Church when in his advent he himself present in the flesh spoke to it words of faith and love and peace.'[265]

One thing we can do is to return to and marvel in the incarnation which brings hope in all circumstances to all humankind. This is something to sing about.

Secondly, and importantly, this 'kiss' has meant the feeling of fire and filling with the Holy Spirit – an experience of Union with Christ. Scottish preacher James Durham (b. 1622) explores this in his great commentary on the Song:

> kisses we understand most lovely friendly sensible manifestations of his love. Let him who is the most excellent and singular person in the world kiss ME a contemptible creature redeemed![266]

Another five hundred years and another commentator, James Pennington, continues:

> What is the kiss of your mouth? It is where the human and divine become completely one. How much we struggle with the belief that you divine lover really love this poor little human so plagued with sin and infidelity: O give me the kisses of your mouth![267]

Back in medieval times, Bernard de Clairvaux extends his interpretation:

> True it may be I am fulfilling the commandments in one way or another, but 'my soul is like earth without water' (Psalm 142.6). Therefore, if my whole offering is to become worthy, let him I pray and beseech 'kiss me with the kisses of his mouth'.[268]

He felt that this image related to refreshment for the one who is fulfilling the commandments, trying to obey the devout life, but utterly dry.

This is a way of seeing that leads into a mystical experience of God. I have sometimes wondered whether a reluctance to embrace theologically the manifest experience of sealing or filling by the Holy Spirit, or – to put it more poetically – the Divine Kiss of the Holy Spirit, is responsible for the reluctance of some to dare to read the Song of Songs allegorically. It is just too challenging in terms of emotional vulnerability.

C. H. Spurgeon came across similar reticence in his day. In his sermon on Songs 1.7, 'Love to Jesus', he says:

> Let him kiss me with the kisses of his lips, for his love is better than wine. 'No,' you say, 'that is too familiar for me.' Then I fear you do not love him, for love is always familiar. Faith may stand at a distance, for her look is saving. But love comes near, for she must kiss, she must embrace. Why, Beloved, sometimes the Christian so loves his Lord that his language becomes unmeaning to the ears of others who have never been in his state. Love has a celestial tongue of her own and I have sometimes heard her speak so that men have said, 'That man rants and raves – he knows not what he says.' Hence it is that love often becomes a Mystic and speaks in mystic language, into which the stranger intrudes not.[269]

So we are at the border here between the doctrines of Evangelical Assurance and the experience of Union with Christ. This is Charismatic Mysticism. As we have seen, it is a rich vein of tradition from the Fathers through the medieval commentators to the Puritans; through the encounter of Pascal, the language of affection in the eighteenth-century 'Love Feasts' of Whitefield's and Wesley's day, on to Finney and Spurgeon, preachers of the nineteenth century and into modern-day Pentecostalism as well as catholic contemplatives who are hungry for, and indeed have experienced, this presence or 'kiss' of God.

The theme of the Kisses of God linked to the Song could be said to answer three cries of humankind. First, an existential cry to know the love of God and his nearness and dearness. This is a common theme of a generation worldwide waiting and longing for God in the silence, tired of techniques and strategies and seeking authenticity.

Second, the great philosophical cry: it answers the question of the purpose of life. If we get this, no matter what else happens: we 'succeed'– we come home to being lovers of God, in the great mystical tradition: This is our inheritance and what we were made for and, yes, our joy, even in a collapsing culture.

Thirdly, this metaphor and the reality behind it answer the great psychological cry of the human heart: they show how the human heart is healed of alienation and finds happiness.

Saint Ignatius, at the start of the Spiritual Exercises speaks of the goal of our lives being to *praise, reverence and serve God forever*. Ignatian spirituality is becoming more and more popular in our time. The Exercises then also speak, as a consequence of this affection, of appropriate 'Indifference' to other things by comparison. Ignatius challenges us not to desire health over illness, wealth over poverty, honour over dishonour or a long life over a short one. The goal is to lead a life that fulfils the purpose for which God created us. This brings freedom from being reliant on those things for ultimate happiness.[270] This challenge at the start of the Exercises could be the rich subject of another book. But for me it has to do with being somehow 'on song' in our love for God: and discovering how to enter this divine romance.

4

The End of Winter and the Season of Singing

In the Song of Songs, the Kisses of God, the coming of Christ into the world, mark also the end of winter and the start of the 'season of singing'.

> Look! Here he comes,
> leaping across the mountains,
> bounding over the hills.
> My beloved is like a gazelle or a young stag ...
> My beloved spoke and said to me,
> 'Arise, my darling, my beautiful one, come with me.
> See! The winter is past;
> the rains are over and gone.
> Flowers appear on the earth;
>   the season of singing has come ...
> (Song 2.8–12)

The 'young stag', the Christ figure, leaps over mountains of difficulty into the world in his incarnation and this marks the 'end of the world's winter'. We remember the famous image from Narnia, where it is 'always winter and never Christmas' – until Aslan comes.

Then comes the season of singing. Gregory of Nyssa (330–95) interprets this passage:

> But the winter of disobedience dried up its root, the blossom was shaken off and fell to the earth; man was stripped of the beauty of immortality as love became cold ... But then came the One who works in us the springtime of our souls, the One who, when an evil wind was on the sea, said: 'Peace be still!' Once again, our nature began to flourish and be adorned with its own blossoms ... That is why the word says:

'The winter is past, the rain is gone … Flowers appear on the earth and the season for singing has come.'[271]

At the end of our journey, our quest has been to be 'on song' in Life. For the mystical mind, this means coming out of winter and entering the springtime and learning to live life as a lover of God and positioning oneself to experience his love. Dear spiritual friend, once we recognize that the mystical mind is not for the rarified few but for all of us, this can be our experience too.

To sit under the banner of love

Part of the burden of this book has been to encourage contemplation, silence and rest in God. This quiet is such a contrast to so much of today's anxious and distracted cultural context. It is very counter-cultural to 'sit alone in a room'. This is expressed in another famous image used in the Song, namely that of sitting under the apple tree – and being under the banner of his love:

> Like an apple tree among the trees of the forest
> is my beloved among the young men.
> I delight to sit in his shade,
> and his fruit is sweet to my taste.
> Let him lead me to the banquet hall,
> and let his banner over me be love.
> (Song 2.2–3)

To find an apple tree in a dense, airless and spiky forest of pines is miraculously refreshing, Like the Bride with her lover, here before the Lord Jesus we can say: I sit. I renounce my usual relentless running about. We can give up our need to be activists, forever running on the treadmill of modern life – and instead take a Sabbath rest. We can sit down, and be still, saying:

> All honour and glory is my loved one's.
> I can sit in total delight.
> I no longer need to be concerned about what others think of me.
> I sit in the delight of perfect contemplation.[272]

THE CLOUD, THE NIGHT, THE FIRE AND THE SONG

As I have said, in times of Revival many are the stories of the experience of God's 'banner of love'. Sarah Edwards describes her experience of 'the banqueting house':

> I continued in a sweet and lively sense of Divine things, until I retired to rest. That night, which was Thursday night, Jan. 28, 1742 was the sweetest night I ever had in my life ... all night I continued in a constant, clear and lively sense of the heavenly sweetness of Christ's excellent and transcendent love, of his nearness to me, and of my dearness to him; with an inexpressibly sweet calmness of soul in an entire rest in him.[273]

'His banner over me is love' (Songs 2.4) is the evocative phrase that has been the inspiration for a veritable crowd of well-loved songs through the ages. Among the best known are those of Palestrina. This sixteenth-century Italian composer, in the Preface to his great work, says:

> There exists a vast mass of love songs of the poets ... the songs of men ruled by passion ... I blush and grieve to think that once I was of their number. But ... I have mended my ways and now have produced a work which treats of the divine love of Christ and his spouse the soul, the Canticle of Solomon.[274]

Palestrina, the musician of the St John in the Lateran church in Rome, speaks for many in expressing a kind of conversion or 'ordering' in his sexual appetites, helped by a reading of the Song of Songs. The Latin Vulgate translation of this 'banner' verse says: 'He has set love in order in me.' We know he intends us to love him with heart, soul, mind and strength; and to love our neighbour as our self. This is 'setting love in order'. It begins in the love of God the Father for his child and the love of the Bridegroom for his Bride: all the healing we need flows from this. The result is this: that we can contemplate; we can be satisfied in him; we can be seated in the heavenly places.

In the Song of Songs both married and single people alike can discover, overarching everything, intimacy with God. We all may be brought to the point where we are able truly to say: His banner over me is love; he refreshes me with apples; I am faint with love. Then this fascination with God will keep us from being led into other fascinations if they try to lead us away from God.

This is not to say that all this is one simple step. Ronald Rolheiser's *The Holy Longing* has helpful reflections on this. He offers 'four steps to turning our restless incompleteness into a restful solitude' – or to subvert this for our purposes. These are:

- Own your own pain or incompleteness.
- Give up false messianic expectations ('Our life is a short time in expectation in which sadness and joy kiss each other at every moment').
- Go Inward (I would rather say: 'Go under the banner of His love').
- Understand it is a movement that is never made once for all.[275]

The idea of 'rest' finds fulfilment in Jesus, who gives this invitation to his disciples: 'Come to me all who labour and are heavy laden, and I will give you rest. Take my yoke upon you and learn of me, for I am gentle and lowly of heart and you will find rest for your souls' (Matt. 11.28–29).

Teresa of Avila's three-fold process to take us towards 'soul-resting' is 'centring prayer' and we have recommended this: *The Prayer of Recollection*' then *The Prayer of Quiet*, and finally: *Divine Union*. We could call this: *Union and Communion*. This was the title of the commentary on the Song of Songs by the missionary to China, J. Hudson Taylor's.[276] The goal of the Song for him is Communion – and Union.

In a sense this is the meaning of arriving at our 'Song'.

Finding your voice for the Song

As the winter ends and the season of singing comes, Chapter 2 of the Song of Songs, which we have been exploring, ends with this challenge, and I will conclude with it too:

> My dove in the clefts of the rock,
>   in the hiding places on the mountainside,
> show me your face,
>   let me hear your voice;
> for your voice is sweet,
>   and your face is lovely.
> (Song 2.14)

The challenge of these tender words from the Divine Bridegroom is to 'show me your face – let me hear your voice; For your voice is sweet and your face is lovely'.

Many are those who, when faced with the intimacy of the Divine Romance and the challenge to transparency, react by hiding their faces and keeping quiet. It is like a bride who has stopped lifting up her face and speaking to her husband: a sad story.

The reasons for this tendency to hide away in any love relationship may just be to do with upbringing; there may be embarrassment at expressing feelings to others. There may also be low self-esteem, fear of failure or past pain: our own secret history. I have known many for whom the very realization of this frozen behaviour can be enough to lead to action to warm up and be healed. I have been involved in some moving seasons in which people 'come back to their first love' and even learn a new language of love.

Maybe I empathize because this awakening is part of my own story. When my own parents got divorced the news had broken out of the blue and completely shocked me. At the age of 14 I had not been aware of any difficulty in my parents' marriage. I appeared to recover and live well through adolescence. But deep down there were consequences that did not come to the surface until I in turn entered my own marriage. My wife found me almost incapable of expressing feelings. I was gregarious in company, but at home when it came to expressing what was going on under the surface, there was complete silence. My wife could have quoted these words from the Song literally to me: 'My dove in the clefts of the rock, in the hiding places on the mountainside, show me your face, let me hear your voice; for your voice is sweet.' The healing came as she loved me and coaxed me into communication and the frozen winter turned into spring. In a similar way, may the Holy Spirit coax us all back to our destiny – our love relationship with God: which I am calling the Song.

In the divine romance we may experience awe and also shame. The beloved feels her unworthiness to be loved. This is the reaction of those confronted with Theophany in the Bible; whether it is Moses, Joshua, Job, Isaiah, or Jeremiah, it is at times appropriate to be speechless in the Presence. But the voice of God in such times is always, it seems, 'Fear not'. When this 'fear not' is heard, there can then be extreme loquacity: for example, Mary's Magnificat, John's Revelation, the Psalmist's torrent of worship.

This may sound paradoxical when I have been calling for silence and quiet in our wordy world. But as often, both are needed. First the quiet, the presence, the listening and the contemplation. And then expression will follow. In times of trouble and sadness I have found I have lost my voice. But when encounter happens then it is that we can start expressing love again. And love deepens when it is expressed.

The miracle is that the Divine Lover of our souls asks us to lift up our head and to dare to speak. The bride hides herself away and loses her voice. We can hear the voice of the Bridegroom who beckons us to 'Look up!'

Christians or whole churches can learn to show their face and let their voice be heard. If they do (as in a marriage), there will be an exponential advance in the relationship.

Arriving home ...

We have reached the end of our journey.

I believe that in all our stages on the journey, we have been wooed by God.

Through the Cloud of Unknowing we sense his mystery and his loving presence.

During the Dark Night also there is complex territory to climb through, from which we emerge strengthened even in this love story. Absence makes the heart grow stronger as well as fonder. We have learnt to love him even in his absence and reunion is all the sweeter for this part of the journey.

The Fire of Love can then be warming for us all, if we would but let it and seek it. Dear spiritual friend, I pray your heart may be warmed with desire as we have considered these stories of mystical, fiery encounter which happen in every generation. They are also for you in your unfolding journey.

The Eternal Song of the Divine Romance is our destination. It doesn't matter if it is a vocal or a silent song. It may be strong or weak, joyful or lamenting. The calling is to 'come back to our first love'. This is Christ's call to the Church in the book of Revelation. It is Jesus' eternal question expressed to Peter after the betrayal: 'Simon, son of John: Do you love me?' (John 21.16). And it is the entire theme of the Song of Songs, where after the winter, the season of singing comes.

We might ask: is this the order we will travel through these territories? Do they come one after the other? This can certainly be the case. I also believe that they can accompany us simultaneously!

Joy is mingled with sorrow on this earth.

Fire can burn in the rain.

THE CLOUD, THE NIGHT, THE FIRE AND THE SONG

One thing is certain: at the end of time, we will join the eternal song of heaven. Until that day, may we practise. The kingdom of heaven is among us, and within us. So let us live out these things today.

Select Bibliography

Primary texts

The Cloud: A. Spearing, ed., *The Cloud of Unknowing and Other Works*, Penguin Classics, 2001.
The Night: Kieran Kavanaugh, ed., *John of the Cross: Selected Writings*, Classics of Western Spirituality, Paulist Press, 1987.
The Fire: Richard Rolle, *The Fire of Love*, Penguin Classics, 1972.
The Song: Richard Norris, ed., *The Song of Songs: Interpreted by Early Christian and Medieval Commentators (The Church's Bible)*, Eerdmans, 2003.
Blaise Pascal, *Pensées*, Classiques Francais, 1995.
Francis de Sales and Jane de Chantal, *Letters of Spiritual Direction*, Péronne Marie Thibert, trans., Classics of Western Spirituality, Paulist Press 1988.
Gregory of Nyssa, *The Life of Moses*, Abraham Malherbe, ed., Classics of Western Spirituality, Paulist Press, 1978.
Hildegard of Bingen, *Selected Writings*, Mark Atherton, trans., Penguin Classics, 2001.
Julian of Norwich, *Revelations of Divine Love*, A. C. Spearing, ed., Penguin Classics, 1973.
Pseudo-Dionysius, *The Complete Works*, Colm Luibheid, ed., Classics of Western Spirituality, Paulist Press, 1987.
Teresa of Avila, *The Interior Castle or the Mansions*, Kieran Kavanaugh and Otilio Rodriguez, eds, Classics of Western Spirituality, Paulist Press, 1987.

Anthologies

Clément, Olivier, *Roots of Christian Mysticism*, New City, 1993.
McGinn, Bernard, *Essential Writings of Christian Mysticism*, Modern Library, 2006.

Other resources for mysticism and contemplation

Augustine, *Confessions*, trans. Henry Chadwick, Oxford World Classics, 1991
Barnes, Peronel, *Beloved: Understanding Holy Love*, at help@peronal.com.
Barton, Ruth Hailey, *Invitation to Solitude and Silence*, SPCK, 2021.

Bourgeault, Cynthia, *Centring Prayer and Inner Awakening*, Cowley Publication, 2004.
Brueggemann, Walter, *The Psalms and the Life of Faith*, Fortress Press, 1995.
Cleverly, Charlie, *Epiphanies of the Ordinary: Encounters that change lives*, Hodder and Stoughton, 2013.
Cleverly, Charlie, *The Song of Songs: Exploring the Divine Romance*, Hodder and Stoughton, 2015.
Comer, John Mark, *The Ruthless Elimination of Hurry*, Hodder and Stoughton, 2019.
de Sales, Francis, *Introduction to the Devout Life*, Ryan, John, ed., Doubleday, 1950.
Guite, Malcolm, 'John of the Cross', in *Parable and Paradox*, Canterbury Press, 2016.
Guyon, Jeanne, *The Autobiography of Madam Guyon*, Thomas Taylor Allen, trans. Kegan Paul, 1897.
Guyon, Jeanne, *Experiencing the Depths of Jesus Christ*, Sowers of Seed, 1981.
Holmes Anne C., *Creative Repair*, SCM, 2023.
Laird, Martin, *Into the Silent Land: The practice of contemplation*, Darton, Longman and Todd, 2006.
McColman, Carl, *The New Big Book of Christian Mysticism*, Broadleaf Books, 2023.
Merton, Thomas, *Contemplative Prayer*, Darton, Longman and Todd, 1995.
Moore, Thomas, *Dark Nights of the Soul*, Piatkus, 2004.
Myss, Caroline, *Entering the Castle*, Simon and Shuster, 2007.
Nouwen, Henri, *The Way of the Heart: Solitude, Silence and Prayer*, Darton, Longman and Todd, 1981.
O'Leary, Brian, *Ignatius Loyola: Christian Mystic*, Messenger Publications, 2023.
Robertson, David, *Cloud Devotion: Through the year with the Cloud of Unknowing*, Paraclete Publishing, 2019.
Soelle, Dorothy, *The Silent Cry: Mysticism and resistance*, Fortress Press, 2001.
Spurgeon, C. H., 1864, *The Most Holy Place*, Christian Focus, 1996.
Starr, Mirabai, *Dark Night of the Soul*, new trans. and intro., Riverhead Books, 2014.
Teresa of Avila, *The Life of Teresa of Jesus: The Autobiography of Teresa of Avila*, E. Alison Peers, trans., Bantam Doubleday, 1996.
Underhill, Evelyn, *Mysticism: A Study in the Nature and Development of Spiritual Consciousness*, 1911.
Underhill, Evelyn, *Practical Mysticism: A Little Book for Normal People*, Wildside Press, 1914.
von Balthasar, Hans Urs, *Prayer (The Act, the Object and the Tensions of Contemplation)*, Ignatius Press, 1986.
Williams, Mark, and Danny Pelman, *Mindfulness: Finding peace in a fractured world*, Piatkus, 2011.
Williams, Rowan, *Silence and Honeycakes: The Wisdom of the Desert*, Lion Publishing, 2003.

Endnotes

1 Pierre Teilhard de Chardin, quoted in *Time Magazine*, 1988.

2 Karl Rahner, 'Christian Living Formerly and Today', essay, 1960, based on a longer treatment in Harvey D. Egan, *Karl Rahner: Mystic of Everyday Life*, Crossroad, 1998, at https://www.theway.org.uk/back/522egan.pdf (accessed 15.1.25).

3 Henry Nouwen, *In the Name of Jesus*, Crossroad, 1989, p. 43.

4 Dorothy Soelle, *The Silent Cry*, Augsburg Fortress, 2001, p. 21. Here she is paraphrasing William James, *The Varieties of Religious Experience*, New York Modern Library, 1921, p. 242ff.

5 Simon Critchley, *On Mysticism: The Experience of Ecstasy*, Profile Books, 2024.

6 Evelyn Underhill, *Practical Mysticism*, Wildside Press, 1914, p. 100.

7 YouTube interview with Speak Life 2019. Tom Holland is the author of *Dominion* (Little, Brown, 2019), and leads the popular podcast 'The Rest is History'.

8 *'The Cloud of Unknowing* (author unknown, c.1380); *The Dark Night of the Soul* (John of the Cross, sixteenth century); *Revelations of Divine Love* (Julian of Norwich, fourteenth century); *The Fire of Love* (Richard Rolle, fourteenth century); The Song of Songs (see, for example, Bernard de Clairvaux's sermons and comments, twelfth century).

9 A. Spearing, ed., *The Cloud of Unknowing and Other Works*, Penguin Classics, 2001, p. 21.

10 Spearing, *The Cloud of Unknowing*, p. 22.

11 John of the Cross, 'The Ascent of Mount Carmel', in Kieran Kavanaugh, ed., *John of the Cross: Selected Writings*, Classics of Western Spirituality, Paulist Press, 1987, p. 5.

12 The fourteenth century is known as the 'Golden Age of English Mysticism' because of the writings of four giants of contemplation: the author of *The Cloud of Unknowing*, Julian of Norwich, Richard Rolle and Walter Hilton.

13 Richard Rolle, *The Fire of Love*, Penguin Classics, 1972, p. 45.

14 Allister Sparks and Desmond Tutu, *Tutu: The Authorised Portrait*, Pan Macmillan, 2011, p. 233.

15 Rolle, *The Fire of Love*, p. 113.

16 Julian of Norwich, *Revelations of Divine Love*, Sixth Revelation, Ch. 14, p. 85.

17 Martin Laird, *Into the Silent Land: The Practice of Contemplation*, Darton, Longman and Todd, 2006.

18 Henri Nouwen returned again and again to this 'life theme' of the necessity of silence for the spiritual life. See particularly Henri Nouwen, *The Way of the Heart: The Spirituality of the Desert Fathers and Mothers*, Darton, Longman and Todd, 1981.

19 'Tout le malheur des hommes vient d'une seule chose: qui est de ne savoir pas demeurer en repos dans une chambre', in Blaise Pascal, *Pensées*, Classiques Français, 1995, p. 58.

20 Spearing, *The Cloud of Unknowing*, p. 20.

21 Spearing, *The Cloud of Unknowing*, p. 92.

22 In Augustine: Homiliy 4 on First John. Implicit in this is that true desire for God stretches us, makes us want what he wants and so grow in Christ-likeness.

23 Spearing, *The Cloud of Unknowing*, p. 21.

24 Henri Nouwen, *In the Name of Jesus: Reflections on Christian Leadership*, Darton, Longman and Todd, 1989.

25 Spearing, *The Cloud of Unknowing*, p. 22.

26 See, for example, David Robertson, *Cloud Devotion: Through the Year with the Cloud of Unknowing*, Paraclete Publishing, 2019; Ana Salto Sánchez del Corrall, *Female Authorship: The Cloud of Unknowing*, Malaga University, 2021.

27 Spearing, *The Cloud of Unknowing*, pp. 21, 26.

28 Spearing, *The Cloud of Unknowing*, p. 22.

29 Spearing, *The Cloud of Unknowing*, p. 47.

30 Spearing, *The Cloud of Unknowing*, p. 24.

31 'Movement', in Ignatius' *Spiritual Exercises* (1534). He taught that spiritual consolation is our experience 'when some interior movement in the soul is caused, through which the soul comes to be inflamed with love of its Creator and Lord', and that we can learn to be aware of and recognize these.

32 Spearing, *The Cloud of Unknowing*, p. 37.

33 Spearing, *The Cloud of Unknowing*, p. 52.

34 See Charlie Cleverly, *Epiphanies of the Ordinary: Encounters that Change Lives*, Hodder and Stoughton, 2013.

35 Originally published in *'The Twelve Steps and the twelve traditions'* Alcoholics Anonymous, 1953.

36 See Teresa of Avila (1515–82), *The Life of Teresa of Jesus: The Autobiography of Teresa of Avila*, E. Alison Peers, trans. and ed., Bantam Doubleday, 1996; Teresa of Avila, *The Interior Castle or the Mansions*, Kieran Kavanaugh and Otilio Rodriguez, eds, Classics of Western Spirituality, Paulist Press, 1979.

37 Hans Urs von Balthasar, *'Prayer – (the Act, the Object and the Tensions of Contemplation)*, Ignatius Press, 1986, p. 38.

38 Spearing, *The Cloud of Unknowing*, p. 67.

39 Johannes Tauler, 'Die predigten Taulers', in Bernard McGinn, *Essential Writings of Christian Mysticism*, Modern Library, 2006, p. 383.

40 Mark Williams and Danny Penman, *Mindfulness: A Practical Guide to Finding Peace in a Frantic World*, Piatkus, 2011.

41 John Mark Comer, *The Ruthless Elimination of Hurry: How to Stay Emotionally Healthy and Spiritually Alive in the Chaos of the Modern World*, Hodder and Stoughton, 2019, p. 140.

42 See 'Mindfulness – a Christian Approach', at Focus on the Family, 2019, at https://www.focusonthefamily.com/family-qa/mindfulness-a-christian-approach/ (accessed 2.2.25); Tim Keller, 'Keller on Quiet Times, Mysticism, and the Priceless Payoff of Prayer', Matt Smethurst Interview, Christian Living, 21 October 2014, at https://www.thegospelcoalition.org/article/tim-keller-on-prayer/ (accessed 2.1.25).

43 Spearing, *The Cloud of Unknowing*, p. 29.

44 Spearing, *The Cloud of Unknowing*, p. 29.

45 Scriptures in this section are from Song of Songs 2.8, 6.3; Mark 1.11; and Romans 9.25.

46 'Mystical Theology', in McGinn, *Essential Writings*, p. 287.

47 Nouwen, *The Way of the Heart*, p. 49.

48 Thomas Merton, *The Wisdom of the Desert*, New Directions Publishing, 1960, p. 3.

49 See, for example, Ruth Hailey Barton, *Invitation to Solitude and Silence*, SPCK, 2014.

50 See also 'Silence and Solitude', in Comer, *The Ruthless Elimination*, p. 119ff; Laird, *Into the Silent Land*, p. 24.

51 'Mystical Theology', in McGinn, *Essential Writings*, p. 287.

52 Richard Foster, *Prayer: Finding the Heart's True Home*, Hodder and Stoughton, 2008, p. 168.

53 Spearing, *The Cloud of Unknowing*, Ch. 17.

54 Thomas Merton, *New Seeds of Contemplation*, New Directions, 1961, p. 5.

55 Spearing, *The Cloud of Unknowing*, p. 127.

56 Spearing, *The Cloud of Unknowing*, p. 55.

57 Spearing, *The Cloud of Unknowing*, p. 26.

58 See McGinn, *Essential Writings*, p. 282.

59 See Charlie Cleverly, *The Discipline of Intimacy: The Joy and Awe of Walking with God*, David C. Cook, 2020, p. 63ff.

60 He is generally known as Pseudo-Dionysius to differentiate him from the early Christian convert in Athens.

61 Dionysius, `Divine Names' I,1, in Olivier Clément, *Roots of Christian Mysticism*, New City, 1983, p. 26.

62 'Mystical Theology', Ch. 4, in McGinn, *Essential Writings*, p. 288.

63 In Soelle, *The Silent Cry*, p. 69.

64 'Mystical Theology', in McGinn, *Essential Writings*, p. 288.

65 'Book of Privy Counselling', Ch. 6, in Spearing, *Cloud of Unknowing*, p. 117.

66 'Book of Privy Counselling', Ch. 6, in Spearing, *Cloud of Unknowing*, p. 117.

67 In Kavanaugh, *Selected Writings*, pp. 55–6.

68 'Most people lead lives of quiet desperation – What is called resignation is confirmed desperation. From the desperate city, you go to the desperate country, and have to console yourself with the bravery of minks and muskrats.' Henry David Thoreau, *Walden* (1854), Black and White Classics, 2014.

69 See Ben Judah, *This is Europe: The Way We Live Now*, Picador, 2023.

70 J. R. R Tolkien, *The Return of the King*, George, Allen and Unwin, 1955.

71 John Garth, *Tolkien and the Great War*, HarperCollins, 2003.

72 Thomas Moore, *Dark Nights of the Soul*, Piatkus, 2004.

73 Jeanne Guyon, *The Autobiography of Madam Guyon*, Thomas Taylor Allen, trans., Kegan Paul, 1897.

74 Spearing, *The Cloud of Unknowing*, Ch, 3.

75 Underhill, *Practical Mysticism: A Little Book for Normal People*, p. 100.

76 This image and interpretation of John's story are from Mirabai Starr, 'Emancipation', in *Oneing*, Journal of the Centre for Action and Contemplation, 2015, at https://store.cac.org/products/oneing-emancipation-pdf-download (accessed 2.1.25).

77 Thanks for some of these insights to Mirabai Starr, *Dark Night of the Soul*, new translation and Introduction, Riverhead Books, 2014.

78 See 'Part 4: The Song' of this book for more; and for a verse-by-verse commentary on the Song of Songs see Charlie Cleverly, 'Understanding the Song', in *The Song of Songs: Exploring the Divine Romance*, Hodder and Stoughton, 2015, pp. 15–30.

79 More thanks to Mirabai Starr for some of these insights.

80 Malcolm Guite, 'John of the Cross', in *Parable and Paradox*, London: Canterbury Press, 2016.

81 Kavanaugh, *Selected Writings*, p. 201.

82 Kavanaugh, *Selected Writings*, p. 186.

83 Kavanaugh, *Selected Writings*, p. 187.

84 John of the Cross, 'The Dark Night', Book 2, Ch. 5, Kavanaugh, *Selected Writings*, p. 203.

85 John of the Cross, 'The Dark Night', Book 2, Ch. 5, Kavanaugh, *Selected Writings*, p. 201.

86 John of the Cross, 'The Dark Night', Book 2, Ch. 5, author's translation, see Kavanaugh, *Selected Writings*.

87 John of the Cross, 'The Dark Night', Book 2, Ch. 5, author's translation, see Kavanaugh, *Selected Writings*, p. 200.

88 Pascal, *Pensées*, p. 69 (my translation: what Pascal called 'diversions' (divertissements) I have here translated 'distractions').

89 Neil Postman, *Amusing Ourselves to Death: Public Discourse in the Age of Show Business*, Methuen Publishing, 1985; Rehan Khan, *Distracting Ourselves to Death: How to Find Purpose in a Bewildering Digital World*, Passionpreneur Publishing, 2021.

90 'The Dark Night', Ch. 11, in Kavanaugh, *Selected Writings*, p. 188.

91 In Kavanaugh, *Selected Writings*, pp. 55–6.

92 John of the Cross, 'Spiritual Canticle', Comment on Stanza 22, 'The Bride has entered'. Kavanaugh, *Selected Writings*, pp. 255–9.

93 Teresa of Avila, quoted in Underhill, *Mysticism*, p. 101.

94 The phrase 'good art compresses the coal of truth into diamonds' is from Erich Auerbach, *Mimesis: The Representation of Reality in Western Literature*, Princeton, 1953.

95 Underhill, *Practical Mysticism*, p. 25.

96 Underhill, *Practical Mysticism*, p. 25.

97 See Kavanaugh *Selected writings of St John of the Cross*, p. 56 (author's paraphrase).

98 John of the Cross, 'Spiritual Canticle', comment on Stanza 22: 'The Bride has entered', in Kavanaugh, *Selected Writings*, pp. 255ff.

99 John of the Cross, 'Spiritual Canticle', vv. 1, 5, 6, in Kavanaugh, *Selected Writings*, p. 221.

100 See *Monty Python's Life of Brian* for one of the first examples of this 'comic ghosting'.

101 Jean-Paul Sartre, *Words*, Penguin Classics, 2000.

102 Both Brecht and Sartre found in communism a new hope only to become disillusioned as it fell to pieces under the brutality of Stalin.

103 Albert Camus, *Notebooks*, 1951–1959. Paragon House, 1991.

104 Albert Camus, 'Return to Tipasa', in *The Myth of Sisyphus*, Vintage 2018.

105 Denis Alexander and Alister McGrath, *Coming to Faith Through Dawkins: 12 Essays on the Pathway from New Atheism to Christianity*, Kregel, 2023, particularly Andy Gosler, Ch. 5, 'Hearing God through Enchantment with Nature'.

106 Maya Angelou, *Wouldn't Take Nothing for My Journey Now*, Virago, 1995.

107 Makoto Fujimura and N. T. Wright, *Art and Faith: A Theology of Making*, Yale University Press, 2021, p. 6.

108 John of the Cross, 'The Dark Night', in Kavanaugh, *Selected Writings*, pp. 56–7.

109 Thomas Moore, *Dark Nights of the Soul*, Piatkus, 2004, p. 189.

110 Moore, *Dark Nights*, p. 195.

111 Anne C. Holmes, *Creative Repair: Pastoral Care and Creativity*, SCM Press, 2023.

112 Underhill, *Practical Mysticism*, p, 23.

113 Underhill, *Practical Mysticism*, p. 25.

114 Christopher Wright, *The Message of Lamentations: Honest to God*, InterVarsity Press, 2015.

115 This phrase comes from an article by Ayla Lepin, 'All things in God', *Church Times*, 31 March, 2023.

116 In Pete Greig, Lectio 365, 5 August 2024, https://www.24-7prayer.com (accessed 15.1.25).

117 Hildegard of Bingen, 'Letter to Guibert of Gembloux', in Mark Atherton, trans, *Hildegard of Bingen: Selected Writings*, Penguin Classics, 2001.

118 Hildegard of Bingen, 'Book of Divine Works' in Atherton, *Hildegard* p. 172.

119 John of the Cross, 'Spiritual Canticle', vv. 15, 16, 20, in Kavanaugh, *Selected Writings* p. 223.

120 Thoreau, *Walden*.

121 Dianne Bergant, *The Song of Songs – the Love Poetry of Scripture*, New City Press, 1998, p. 40.

122 John of the Cross, in Kavanaugh, *Selected Writings*.

123 Gerard Manley Hopkins, 'God's Grandeur', in *The Major Works*, Oxford World Classics, 2009.

124 Gerard Manley Hopkins, 'God's Grandeur'.

125 Gerard Manley Hopkins, 'God's Grandeur'.

126 *New York Times*, 12 July 2018.

127 Hopkins, 'As Kingfishers Catch Fire', in *Major Works*, p. 129.

128 Underhill, *Practical Mysticism*.

129 Underhill, *Practical Mysticism*, p. 12.

130 Rainer Maria Rilke, 'The Vast Night', in S. Mitchell, trans., *Poems to the Night*, 1916.

131 Wendell Berry, 'The Peace of Wild Things', in *The Peace of Wild Things*, Penguin, 2018. Copyright © Wendell Berry, 1964, 1968, 1970, 1973, 1977, 1980, 1982, 1994, 1999, 2005, 2016. Reprinted by permission of Penguin Books Limited.

132 John Burger, *Teresa of Avila and John of the Cross: A Friendship that Defies Expectations*, Aleteia, 2020, https://aleteia.org/2020/07/06/teresa-of-avila-and-john-of-the-cross-a-friendship-that-defies-expectations (accessed 2.2.25).

133 Some of this description comes from: https://pilgrimsprogresspddm.blogspot.com/2012/11/the-icon-of-friendship.html (accessed 2.2.25).

134 Article, 2024, at https://www.catholicireland.net.

135 Wendy M. Wright, ed., *Francis de Sales and Jane de Chantal: Letters of Spiritual Direction*, Classics of Western Spirituality, Paulist Press, 1988.

136 Wright, *Francis de Sales*, p. 34.

137 Wright, *Francis de Sales*, p. 3.

138 Wright, *Francis de Sales*, p. 4.

139 Wright, *Francis de Sales*, p. ?? check with au.

140 Wright, *Francis de Sales*, pp. 4–5.

141 Wright, *Francis de Sales*; for this summary of spirituality see the 'Six Themes' identified in the Introduction.

142 Wright, *Francis de Sales*, pp. 128–9.

143 Wright, *Francis de Sales*, p. 141.

144 Wright, *Francis de Sales*, pp. 202ff.

145 Wright, *Francis de Sales*, p. 76.

146 R. S. Thomas, 'The Bright Field', *Collected Poems*, Phoenix, 1993. Reproduced with permission of Orion Publishing Group, Ltd through PLSclear.

147 Teresa of Avila, *The Interior Castle*, Kavanaugh and Rodriguez, eds.

148 R. S. Thomas, 'The Bright Field'. Reproduced with permission of Orion Publishing Group, Ltd through PLSclear.

149 Spearing, *Cloud of Unknowing*, p. 107.

150 Teresa of Avila, *The Interior Castle*.

151 Luke 17.21, KJV, and alternative translations of the NIV and ESV.

152 Augustine, *Confessions* (tr. Henry Chadwick), Oxford World Classics 1991.

153 'Augustine's impact on Western Christian thought can hardly be overstated; only his beloved example Paul of Tarsus has been more influential, and Westerners have generally seen Paul through Augustine's eyes', Diarmaid MacCulloch, *A History of Christianity: The First Three Thousand Years*, Penguin, 2010.

154 Thomas Keating, the Cistercian founder of one contemporary Centring Prayer movement, traces the roots of Centring Prayer to the Desert Fathers as well as to the *Lectio Divina* tradition of Benedictine monasticism, but especially to works like *The Cloud of Unknowing* and the writings of Teresa and John of

the Cross. Then the influence of Thomas Merton in the twentieth century is also behind the contemporary Centring Prayer movement and renewed Christian interest in contemplative practices. Merton's theology attempted to unify the tenets of Christianity with other philosophical trends including existentialism. In this context, he was an advocate of contemplative prayer without words (technical term – 'non discursive').

155 Teresa of Avila, *The Interior Castle*, p. 39.
156 Teresa of Avila, *The Way of Perfection*, E. Allison Peers, ed. and trans., Dover Thrift Edition, 2012, Ch. 28, p. 150.
157 Teresa of Avila, *The Way of Perfection*, Ch. 28, p. 150.
158 Teresa of Avila, *The Way of Perfection*, Ch. 28, p. 152.
159 Teresa of Avila, *The Way of Perfection*, Ch. 28, p. 153.
160 Teresa of Avila, *The Interior Castle*, Fourth Mansion, Ch. 2, p. 74.
161 Teresa of Avila, *The Interior Castle*, Sixth Mansion, p. 118.
162 Teresa of Avila, *The Interior Castle*, Fifth Mansion, Ch. 31, p. 165.
163 Teresa of Avila, *The Interior Castle*, Fifth Mansion, Ch. 31, p. 165.
164 Teresa of Avila, *The Interior Castle*, Fifth Mansion, Ch. 31, p. 165.
165 Teresa of Avila, *The Interior Castle*, Fifth Mansion, Ch. 31, p. 166.
166 Or 'placed me' I think she says.
167 Teresa of Avila, *The Interior Castle*, Fifth Mansion, Ch. 1, p. 90.
168 Julian of Norwich, *Revelations of Divine Love*, A. C. Spearing, ed., Penguin Classics, 1973, Ch. 12, p. 83.
169 Julian of Norwich, *Revelations of Divine Love*, Ch. 86, p. 211.
170 Julian of Norwich, *Revelations of Divine Love*, Ch. 54, p. 157.
171 Julian of Norwich, *Revelations of Divine Love*, Ch. 54, p. 157.
172 Julian of Norwich, *Revelations of Divine Love*, Ch. 54, p. 158.
173 Teresa of Avila, Seventh Mansion, p. 179.
174 Teresa of Avila, *The Interior Castle*, Seventh Mansion, p. 179.
175 See Barton, *Invitation to Solitude and Silence* for a helpful guide.
176 Article in *The Week*, June 2024.
177 Julian of Norwich, *Revelations of Divine Love*, Alison Spearing and Elizabeth Spearing, eds, Penguin Classics, 1998. p. 66.
178 All these phrases are from the final pagers of Teresa's *The Interior Castle*, pp. 184–94.
179 T. S. Eliot, 'Murder in the Cathedral', in *Collected Poems: 1909–1962*, Faber and Faber, 1969.
180 Paagiotis Kantarzis, 'Eastern Orthodox Theology', Christian Focus 2021 is a helpful monograph written by a friend and evangelical pastor in Athens who has been 'looking for his brothers' in the Orthodox, Church for many years – and finding them!
181 T. S. Eliot, 'Little Gidding', 'The Four Quartets', in *Collected Poems: 1909–1962*.
182 Hildegard of Bingen, (Scivias II Vision 1) in Atherton, *Selected Writings*.
183 Rolle, *The Fire of Love*, p. 45.
184 The references are: Exodus 3.2, 13.21, 24.17; Song of Songs 8.6; Ezekiel 1.4ff; Matthew 3.11; Hebrews 12.29; Luke 12.29.

185 This is because of the writings of four giants of contemplation: the author of *The Cloud of Unknowing*, Julian of Norwich, Richard Rolle and Walter Hilton.
186 Rolle, *The Fire of Love*, 'Prologue'.
187 Rolle, *The Fire of Love*, Ch. 16.
188 I was helped in this summary biography by James Ford's article in *patheos.com*, 20 Jan. 2024, at https://www.patheos.com/blogs/monkeymind/2024/01/richard-rolles-fire-of-love.html (accessed 2.2.25).
189 Evelyn Underhill, *Mysticism: A Study in the Nature and Development of Spiritual Consciousness*, 1911.
190 Evelyn Underhill, The Mysticism of Richard Rolle, at https://thevalueofsparrows.wordpress.com/2017/09/20/mysticism-the-mysticism-of-richard-rolle-by-evelyn-underhill/ (accessed 24.4.25).
191 Rolle, *The Fire of Love*, p. 88.
192 I'm drawing on Underhill, *Practical Mysticism*, for some of this summary.
193 Rolle, *The Fire of Love*, Ch. 16.
194 Rolle, *The Fire of Love*, Ch.17.
195 Song of Songs 5.8, KJV, 8.6.
196 Rolle, The Fire of Love, Ch. 17, p. 99.
197 Kavanaugh, *Selected Writings*, p. 294.
198 John of the Cross, 'Living Flame of Love', in Kavanaugh, *Selected Writings* pp. 292ff.
199 English translation: 'You are the fairest of all the Sons of men / You cover me with your love / and the grace flowing from your lips is balm to my life and a healing balm of love / and I am lovesick, faint with love', Elisabeth Boubouze, *Tu es le plus beau*, Louange Traduction Composition (LTC), 1996.
200 Teresa of Avila, 1577, *The Life of St Teresa of Jesus by Herself*, J. Cohen, trans., Penguin Classics, 2004.
201 For more on this discussion see Cleverly, *The Song of Songs*, pp. 15–30; and Denys Turner, *Eros and Allegory*, Cistercian Publishing, 1995.
202 Spearing, *The Cloud of Unknowing*, Ch. 26.
203 Guyon, *The Autobiography*, pp. 36.
204 Jeanne Guyon, *Experiencing the Depths of Jesus Christ*, Sowers of Seed, 1981, p. 23.
205 T. S. Eliot, 'Little Gidding', 'The Four Quartets', in *Collected Poems: 1909–1962*, 2002, Faber & Faber.
206 'The Waste Land' was published shortly after the First World War in 1922 and 'Four Quartets' towards the end of the Second in 1943; Eliot, *Collected Poems 1909–1962*.
207 Julian of Norwich, *Revelations of Divine Love*, Penguin Classics, 1973, p. 211.
208 Julian of Norwich, *Revelations of Divine Love*, Ch. 86, p. 211.
209 Eliot, 'Little Gidding', p. 196ff.
210 Rolle, *The Fire of Love*, Ch. 17, p. 99.
211 Rolle, *The Fire of Love*, Ch. p. 100.
212 Joseph de Beaufort was an abbot who collected Brother Lawrence's letters and interviews to create *The Practice of the Presence of God*, Hodder and Stoughton, 1981.

213 George Fox, *Journal*, Axios Press, 2012, p. 23.
214 This 'Testament' is placed at the beginning of Pascal, *Pensées*, p. xxx.
215 Underhill, *Mysticism,* p. 190.
216 Pascal's 'Memorial', at https://www.ccel.org/ccel/pascal/memorial.i.htm (accessed 3/1/25).
217 George Fox, *Journal*, p. 23.
218 Jonathan Edwards: 'Some thoughts concerning the present Revival of Religion in New England', Gale Ecco Print, 2010.
219 Charles Finney (1876), Helen Wessel, *The Autobiography of Charles G. Finney*, Bethany House, 2006.
220 'History of American Christianity', at https://www.christianleaders.org/course/view.php?id=1485 (accessed 15.1.25).
221 Underhill, *Mysticism*, p. 176.
222 St Francis and St Ugolino di Monte Santa Maria, *The Little Flowers of Saint Francis*, Vintage Spiritual Classics, 1998, Ch. 13.
223 Shawn Stevens, *An Overview of the Azusa Street Revival*, Zion Christian Ministries, 2003.
224 Stanley Frodsham, *With Signs Following*, Gospel Publishing House, 1941.
225 Cecil M. Robeck, *The Azusa Street Mission And Revival: The Birth Of The Global Pentecostal Movement*, Thomas Nelson, 2006; Pew Forum on Religion and Public Life, 5 October 2006, at https://www.pewresearch.org/religion/2006/10/05/pew-forum-on-religion-amp-public-life-releases-results-from-a-10-country-public-opinion-survey-of-pentecostals/ (accessed 2.2.25).
226 Soelle, *The Silent Cry.*
227 Personal letter to the author.
228 Augustine, 'Homily 4 on the First Epistle of John', at https://www.newadvent.org/fathers/170209.htm (accessed 2.2.25).
229 François Fénelon, quoted in R. Arthur Matthews, *Born for Battle*, Overseas Missionary Fellowship, 1978, p. 115.
230 Underhill, *Mysticism*, p. 176.
231 Tom Holland, YouTube interview with Speak Life, 2019, at https://www.youtube.com/playlist?list=PL4zD5797LHdfuwEIuCxpVz7BBnoU3CTiO (accessed 2.1.25).
232 R. S. Thomas, 'A Blackbird Singing', *Collected Poems*, Phoenix, 1993. Reproduced with permission of Orion Publishing Group, Ltd through PLSclear.
233 Eleanor Farjeon, 'Morning has Broken' © Eleanor Farjeon, 1931, in Percy Dearmer, Martin Shaw and Ralph Vaughan Williams, eds, *Songs of Praise*, Oxford University Press, 1931. Reproduced by kind permission by David Higham Associates.
234 C. S. Lewis, *The Magician's Nephew*, The Bodley Head, 1955; J. R. R. Tolkien, *The Silmarillion*, George Allen and Unwin, 1977.
235 The references in this paragraph are found in Underhill, *Mysticism*, p. 440.
236 Stacy Horn article, *Time* magazine, 13 August 2013, at https://ideas.time.com/2013/08/16/singing-changes-your-brain/ (accessed 2.2.15).
237 Hopkins 'Spring', *The Major Works*, p. 130.
238 'Cædmon's Hymn', trans. Jamie Fishwick-Ford, reproduced with permission of the President and Fellows of Magdalen College, Oxford, https://www.

magd.ox.ac.uk/blog/bedes-ecclesiastical-history-and-caedmons-hymn/ (accessed 3.1.25).

239 Owen Hopkin, Hildegard of Bingen, *Article for Classic FM.com*, at https://www.classicfm.com/composers/bingen/guides/discovering-great-composers-hildegard-von-bingen/ (accessed 2.1.25).

240 Hildegard of Bingen, Symphonia Caelestium Revelationum, p, 116.

241 Underhill, *Mysticism*, p. 440.

242 Matthew Phillips, 'Martin Luther on Music', 2014, at https://wp.cune.edu/matthewphillips/2014/06/01/martin-luther-on-music/ (accessed 3.1.25).

243 Preface to Calvin's Genevan Psalter 1565, at https://www.ccel.org/ccel/ccel/eee/files/calvinps.htm (accessed 3.1.25).

244 A. W. Tozer, *Worship: The Missing Jewel in the Evangelical Church*, Christian Publications, 1992.

245 Don Williams, 'Charismatic Worship', in Nick Drake, 'A Theology for Pentecostal-Charismatic Worship using Calvin's 'Union with Christ', PhD thesis for the University of Birmingham, at https://etheses.bham.ac.uk/id/eprint/8516/ (accessed 3.1.25).

246 Alasdair MacInytre, *After Virtue: A Study in Moral Theory*, Gerald Duckworth, 2007, argues that this current cultural moment in which we find ourselves is like the fall of the Roman Empire. The West has abandoned reason and the tradition of the virtues ... We are not governed by faith or reason ... but by emotivism.

247 Andrew Peterson / Ben Shive *Is He Worthy?* Capitol Cmg Genesis, Vamos Publishing.

248 'Jesu joy of man's desiring' is the English paraphrase by Myra Hess in 1926 of Bach's four-part setting of the hymn 'Jesu, meiner Seelen Wonne', which had been written by Martin Janus in 1661. The German is already remarkable for the emotion of the lines *Wohl mir, dass ich Jesu habe* (It is well for me that I have Jesus), and again as its tenth movement, *Jesus bleibt meine Freude* (Jesus Remains My Joy).

249 Chris Martin, Coldplay, 'Fix You', *X&Y*, Parlophone Records and Warner Music Group, 2005.

250 Walter Brueggemann, *The Psalms and the Life of Faith*, Fortress Press, 1995, p. 107.

251 Rolle, *The Fire of Love*, p. 113.

252 Julian of Norwich, *Revelations of Divine Love*, Ch. XIV, p. 85.

253 Julian of Norwich, *Revelations of Divine Love*, Ch XXIV.

254 Julian of Norwich, *All Will be Well: 30 Days With a Great Spiritual Teacher*, Ave Maria Press, 2008.

255 Thomas Celano was commissioned by Pope Gregory to write the first biography of St Frances (the 'First Life'), published in 1229.

256 This is the view of Claus Westermann, *Praise and Lament in the Psalms*, Westminster John Knox, 1987.

257 Walter Brueggemann, *The Psalms in the Life of Faith*, Fortress Press, 1995, p. 124.

258 Brueggemann, *The Psalms in the Life of Faith*, p. 119.

259 Bernard began to produce these in 1135, and died with his series, at 86 sermons, incomplete.

260 Spearing, *Cloud of Unknowing*, Ch. 4.

261 C. H. Spurgeon, 'A Bundle of Myrrh', sermon, 1864, in *The Most Holy Place*, Christian Focus, 1996, p. 112.

262 For a verse-by-verse commentary see Charlie Cleverly, *The Song of Songs: Exploring the Divine Romance*, Hodder and Stoughton. 2015.

263 Karl Barth, *Church Dogmatics*, Vol. 3, Part 1, T & T Clark, 2004, p. 313. (Quoted, among others by Eugene Peterson, *5 Smooth Stones for Pastoral Work*, 1996, p. 36).

264 Bernard de Clairvaux, *Sermons on the Song of Songs*, Vol 2, Cistercian Publications 1971, pp. 5, 8, 10.

265 This and subsequent comments from various writers on the Song of Songs in this chapter can be found in Richard Norris, *The Song of Songs Interpreted by Early Christian and Medieval Commentators (The Church's Bible)*, Eerdmans, 2003, p. 21.

266 James Durham, *Song of Solomon*, The Banner of Truth Trust, 1982, p. 74.

267 M. Basil Pennington, *The Song of Songs: A Spiritual Commentary*, Skylight Paths 2004, p. 35.

268 Bernard of Clairvaux, in Norris, *The Song of Songs*, p. 23.

269 Spurgeon, *The Most Holy Place*, p. 70.

270 See *The Spiritual Exercises of St Ignatius of Loyola*, Para 23 Principle and Foundation, Gracewing, 2004, p. 11.

271 Gregory of Nyssa (fourth century), in Richard Norris, *The Song of Songs: Interpreted by Early Christian and Medieval Commentators*, Eerdmans, 2004, p. 122.

272 Pennington, *The Song of Songs*, p. 30.

273 Jonathan Edwards, *The Works of Jonathan Edwards*, Vol. 1, The Banner of Truth Trust, 1974.

274 Matthew O'Donovan, sleeve notes, *Song of Songs*, sung by Stile Antico, Harmonia Mundi.

275 Ronald Rolheiser, *The Holy Longing: The Search for a Christian Spirituality*, Doubleday, 1999, p. 204ff. Rolheiser is quoting from Henri Nouwen, 'Loneliness to Solitude', in *Reaching Out: The Three Movements of the Spiritual Life*, HarperCollins, 1976.

276 J. Hudson Taylor, *Union and Communion*, China Inland Mission, 1914.

www.ingramcontent.com/pod-product-compliance
Lightning Source LLC
Chambersburg PA
CBHW060606080526
44585CB00013B/697